Everyday
Indonesian

Everyday Indonesian

Your Guide to Speaking Indonesian Quickly and Effortlessly in a Few Hours

by Thomas G. Oey, Ph.D

PERIPLUS EDITIONS
Singapore • Hong Kong • Indonesia

Published by Tuttle Publishing, an imprint of Periplus Editions (HK) Ltd.

www.tuttlepublishing.com

Copyright @1992 Periplus Editions (HK) Ltd.

ISBN: 978-0-945971-58-0

Publisher: Eric M. Oey

Design and Production: Peter Ivey

Photographs: Jill Gocher

Distributors by

Indonesia
PT Java Books Indonesia
Kawasan Industri Pulogadung
Jl. Rawa Gelam IV No.9, Jakarta 13930
Tel: (62 21) 4682 1088; Fax: (62 21) 461 0206
cs@javabooks.co.id

Japan
Tuttle Publishing
Yaekari Building, 3rd Floor
5-4-12 Osaki, Shinagawa-ku, Tokyo141 0032
Tel: (81) 3 5437-0171; Fax: (81) 3 5437-0755
sales@tuttle.co.jp
www.tuttle.co.jp

Asia Pacific
Berkeley Books Pte. Ltd.
61 Tai Seng Avenue #02-12 Singapore 534167
Tel: (65) 6280-1330; Fax: (65) 6280-6290
inquiries@periplus.com.sg
www.periplus.com

North America, Latin America & Europe
Tuttle Publishing
364 Innovation Drive
North Clarendon, VT 05759-9436 U.S.A.
Tel: 1 (802) 773-8930; Fax: 1 (802) 773-6993
info@tuttlepublishing.com
www.tuttlepublishing.com

10 11 12 13 14   14 13 12 11 10

Printed in Indonesia

Contents

6

Introduction

Indonesian (*Bahasa Indonesia*) is a relatively new spoken and written dialect of the Malay language, developed by Dutch scholars at the beginning of the 20th century as the standard or "correct" dialect to be taught in the colonial schools. It is an Austronesian (Malayo-Polynesian) tongue of amazing complexity, rich in vocabulary borrowed from Sanskrit, Arabic, Portuguese, Dutch, English, Chinese, Javanese, and many other languages.

A colloquial *pasar* or market form of the language has been in use as the lingua franca throughout the archipelago for several centuries, and is quite simple to learn. This book is intended for first time visitors who wish to gain a working knowledge of colloquial Indonesian. Most visitors will find that a little study of a few words and phrases goes a very long way, and that most Indonesians are very happy to help you learn the language.

The lessons are prioritized, with more important words and phrases being given first, so that you may profit no matter how deeply into the book you go. By studying the first section only, you acquire a basic "survival" Indonesian, and by mastering the first three sections you should be able to get around quite well on your own. In order to present each lesson clearly as a unit, we have found it necessary in some cases to repeat vocabulary.

I do not apologize for preferring colloquial to "standard" or "book" Indonesian here, as this is the common spoken form of the language, and the most readily understood. Care has been taken to include only vocabulary that has immediate practical application for visitors. By repetition and memorization of the materials you will quickly gain a grasp of the language's basic elements. Rather than include long and tedious lists of words and phrases in the lessons themselves, we have appended at the back of the book a miniature bilingual dictionary that should be adequate for the needs of most tourists.

At the end of the book you will also find additional information on the use of verb and noun affixes, and suggestions for further study. Do not be deceived by the claim that "Indonesian has no grammar." As one studies the language in greater depth, one realizes how complex it actually is. After several months or years, you may realize that while you are able to speak the language *cukupan* (sufficiently), it is as difficult as any other language to truly master. In fact the grammar, morphology, and syntax of standard *Bahasa Indonesia* as taught in the schools is at least as complex as any European language!

Thomas G. Oey, Ph.D.
Nashville, Tennessee

Acknowledgements

I would like to thank my brother Eric, who originally suggested that I write this book, made many valuable suggestions, and edited the final manuscript. I would also like to thank my parents, Tom and Berenice; my aunt and uncle in Java, Tante Inggawati and Om Sutantho; the employees of Java Books and Java Engineering, who read portions of the draft and suggested many improvements; and Sudarno Sumarto, who read the draft in its final stages.

An exposed buddha figure stares out from his stupa at Borobudur.

PART ONE

The Basics

Pronunciation

To learn to pronounce the language correctly, ask a native speaker to read aloud some of the examples given in this section. Then try to imitate his or her pronunciation as accurately as you can. Be aware, however, that there are many dialectical variations in Indonesian, some producing very strong accents. Stress also varies from region to region. In Sumatra (and incidentally among the Malays of Malaysia) stress is generally placed on the penultimate syllable, whereas the Javanese and many other Indonesians stress the final syllable of a word.

Unlike English, the spelling of Indonesian is consistently phonetic. Many people say the pronunciation is similar to Spanish or Italian.

Consonants

Most are pronounced roughly as in English. The main exceptions are as follows:

c is pronounced "ch" (formerly spelled "tj")
   cari to look for, seek   ***cinta*** to love

g is always hard, as in "girl"
   guna to use   ***gila*** crazy

h is very soft, and often not pronounced
   habis ⇒ *abis* finished   ***hidup*** ⇒ *idup* to live
   sudah ⇒ *suda* already   ***mudah*** ⇒ *muda* easy
   lihat ⇒ *liat* to see   ***tahu*** ⇒ *tau* to know

kh is found in words of Arabic derivation, and sounds like a hard "k"

    khabar news   **khusus** special

ng is is always soft, as in "hanger"

    dengar to hear   **hilang** lost

ngg is always hard, as in "hunger"

    ganggu to bother   **mangga** mango

r is trilled or rolled, as in Spanish

    ratus hundred   **baru** new

Vowels

As in English, there are five written vowels (a, e, i, o, u) and two diphthongs (ai, au):

a is very short, like the a in "father":

    satu one   **bayar** to pay

e is usually unaccented, like the u in "but":

    empat four   **beli** to buy

When stressed, or at the end of a word, however, *e* sounds like the "é" in "passé":

    desa village   **cabe** chili pepper

i is long like the "ea" in "bean":

    tiga three   **lima** five

o is long, as in "so":

    bodoh stupid   **boleh** may

u is long like the "u" in "humor":

    tujuh seven   **untuk** for

au is like the "ow" in "how":

> ***atau*** or   ***pulau*** island

ai is pronounced like the word "eye":

> ***pantai*** beach   ***sampai*** to reach

Notes:

Under the influence of Javanese, final *ai* is often pronounced like "é" in "passé":

> ***sampai*** ⇒ *sampé* beach

Similarly, final *au* often becomes "o":

> ***hijau*** ⇒ *hijo* green

Under the influence of the Jakarta dialect, final syllable *a* between consonants often becomes a short "e" (shwa):

> ***pintar*** ⇒ *pinter* smart

> ***benar*** ⇒ *bener* true, correct

> ***malas*** ⇒ *males* lazy

Sunrise at Mount Bromo, a spectacular volcanic caldera in East Java.

Greetings

When greeting and taking leave of one another, Indonesians shake hands lightly (not firmly, the way Americans do). Muslims touch the right hand to their heart afterwards as a gesture of goodwill. (Never use the left hand to greet or touch someone.) Kissing, hugging or other physical greetings are never practiced in public.

Selamat is a word used in most Indonesian greetings. It comes from the Arabic *salam*, meaning peace, safety or salvation. By itself, the exclamation *Selamat!* means "Congratulations!" Like English "good," it is followed by the time of day and other words to form most common greetings:

Selamat datang	Welcome (*datang* = to come)
Selamat pagi	Good morning (*pagi* = morning, until 11 am)
Selamat siang	Goodday (*siang* = midday, from 11 am to 3 pm)
Selamat sore	Good afternoon (*sore* = late afternoon, 3 pm to nightfall)
Selamat malam	Good evening (*malam* = night, after dark)
Selamat tidur	Good night (*tidur* = to sleep)

Apa khabar is another common greeting which literally means "What's the news" (*apa* = what, *khabar* = news), or in other words "How are you?" The standard answer is "*Khabar baik*," meaning "I'm fine" (*baik* = well, fine).

You will also find yourself greeted with the following questions, even by complete strangers:

Mau ke mana? (lit: Want-to-where?)	Where are you going?

Dari mana pak/ibu?   Were are you [coming] from?
(lit: From-where-pak/ibu?)

This is said out of curiosity, and the person is usually not all that interested where you are actually going or coming from. This is just another way of saying "Hello!"

You may answer:

Dari [+ place]   From [+ place]

Saya mau ke [+ place] I am going to [+ place]

Jalan-jalan saja.   Just going for a walk.
(lit: Walk-walk-only.)

Makan angin.   Just out for some air.
(lit: Eat-wind.)

Tidak ke mana-mana.   Not anywhere in particular.
(lit: Not-to-where-where.)

When taking leave of someone, it is polite to excuse one-self by saying:

Mari. Saya pergi dulu. Excuse me. I am going now.
(lit: Let's. I-go-first.)   (= Goodbye for now!)

Sampai jumpa lagi.   See you again.
(lit: Until-meet-again.)

More informally, you can also say:

Da-da! or ***Bye-Bye!***   Goodbye (so long!)

Note: *Da!* comes from the Dutch *dag* meaning "day." *Bye-bye* is from English.

If you are the one staying behind, you respond by saying:

Selamat jalan.   "Bon voyage"
(lit: Safe-journey.)

Forms of Address

As in any language, there are many ways of addressing someone in Indonesian. Because Indonesians have a strong sense of social hierarchy, these forms of address often carry with them certain class and other distinctions. It is important therefore to use the appropriate term. Some forms of address are quite "safe" or "neutral" in this regard, and may be used in a wide variety of situations; these are the ones that should be learned first and used most often.

> *Bapak* or *pak* (literally: "father") is the most common way of addressing an adult male in Indonesian. It is used very much like "Mr." or "sir" in English. *Bapak* is always used when addressing older men, and may also be used to address a contemporary or a younger man (although other forms may be used in this case as well, see below).

> *Ibu* or *bu* (literally: "mother") is similarly be used to address all women, particularly older, married women.

Note: *Bapak* and *ibu* are often used followed by the person's first name (not the last name), meaning Mr. or Mrs. so and so. This is quite universal throughout Indonesia, and you can almost never go wrong addressing someone in this way (the only exception may be that when used by a much older person to address a much younger person, it may seem a bit overly formal).

> *Saudara* (literally "brother/sister") is used in more formal situations to address an adult male or female who is about one's own age or a bit younger. This form is more often used to address young, unmarried people than older people, and usually upon meeting someone for the first time or in speeches, etc.

> *Anda* is a term of fairly recent coinage, intended to mean "you" in a neutral way. It is also considered to

be rather formal and is likewise used among young, educated adults who meet for the first time (also in television commercials, etc.).

Kamu and ***engkau*** are pronouns that both mean "you" in a familiar sense (equivalent to *Du* in German or *tu* in French). They are used in informal situations to address close friends, children or social inferiors, but should not generally be used as a substitute for English "you." Once you get to know someone well, you can use their name or the form *kamu* ("you").

Tuan ("sir"), ***nyonya*** ("madam"), and ***nona*** ("miss") are forms that Indonesians will often use to address you. *Tuan* means "my lord" and was used to address aristocrats and Europeans during colonial times. *Nyonya* and *nona* are borrowed from the Portuguese and have a similar connotation of peasants or servants addressing their mistress or patron. You should not use these forms to address Indonesians, even if they address you in this way. Stick to *bapak* or *ibu*.

Sand, surf and swaying palms at Matras Beach on the island of Bangka.

Om ("Uncle") and *tante* ("Aunt") are borrowed from Dutch and are used to address older men or women and foreigners, particularly Chinese. Again, stick to *bapak* and *ibu* when addressing Indonesians, even if the person to whom you are speaking addresses you with these terms.

Mas literally means "older brother" in Javanese, and is a polite form of address for a contemporary or a younger person. It is commonly used in Java to address a waiter, porter or pedicab (*becak*) driver, and hence can have the connotation of addressing a social inferior. When in doubt it is better to stick with *pak*.

Mbak or **sus** are similarly used in Java to summon a waitress or a shopgirl.

Summary

To be on the safe side, always use *bapak* and *ibu* when addressing adults whom you are meeting for the first time (*saudara* and *anda* may also be used by younger people to address their peers). Once you get to know someone better, use *bapak* or *ibu* followed by the person's first name, or simply the first name alone.

The following is a brief dialogue between a foreigner (F) and an Indonesian (I) who works in a hotel.

I:	**Selamat pagi, tuan!**	Good morning, sir.
F:	**Selamat pagi, pak!**	Good morning, *pak*.
I:	**Tuan mau ke mana?**	Where are you going, sir.
F:	**Saya mau ke restoran.**	I am going to the restaurant.

Pronouns

As indicated above, a strong sense of social hierarchy attaches to the personal pronouns for "I" and "you." For this reason, Indonesians prefer to use first names or the polite forms of address given above rather than these personal pronouns. In conversation with someone you are meeting for the first time or meeting on a more formal basis, it is more polite to refer to them as *bapak or ibu* followed by the person's first name (if known) rather than using the pronouns for "you."

	singular	plural
1st person	I **saya, aku**	we **kita, kami**
2nd person	you **anda, saudara, kamu, engkau bapak, ibu**	you all **kalian, saudara sekalian, anda sekalian**
3rd person	he, she, it **dia**	they **mereka**

Note: Indonesian pronouns do not distinguish gender. Thus *dia* may mean he, she or it.

1st person (singular): I **saya, aku**

Use your own name with people who know you, or else the pronoun *saya* (which originally meant "your slave" but now generally means "I"). *Aku* also means "I" but is used in more informal circumstances, as are the Jakarta slang forms *gua* and *gue* (which derive from Hokkien Chinese). Note that when requesting something, words for "I" are often omitted because this is understood.

1st person (plural): we **kita, kami**

Kami means "we" or "us" but formally excludes the person or persons being addressed, whereas *kita* includes the person or persons you are speaking to. In everyday speech, *kita* is in fact used in both contexts and you may generally use this form to translate English "we."

2nd person (singular): you
anda, saudara, kamu, engkau, bapak, ibu

Use *bapak* or *ibu*. In informal circumstances, the first name alone may also be used. If the person being addressed is about the same age as yourself, use *anda* or *saudara*. *Kamu* or *engkau* may be used for children or if you know the person well.

2nd person (plural): you all
kalian, saudara sekalian, anda sekalian

3rd person (singular): he, she, it *dia*

For animate objects and persons use *dia*. The word *beliau* is also used in formal circumstances to refer to a person of very high status who is not present. For inanimate things, use *ini* (this one) or *itu* (that one), to mean "it."

3rd person (plural): they *mereka*

Visitors to the volcanic island of Krakatau document their adventure.

Basic Vocabulary

The following are essential words for basic "survival" Indonesian. We suggest that you make a set of flashcards to help yourself learn them quickly.

tidak	no, not	*ya*	yes
ada	to have, there is	*mau*	to want, wish
bisa	to be able, can	*lihat*	to see
datang	to arrive	*dari*	from
pergi	to go, to leave	*ke*	to, toward
jalan	to walk, travel, street	*di*	in, at
sini	here	*sana*	there
dalam	in	*luar*	out
makan	to eat	*minum*	to drink
beli	to buy	*jual*	to sell
harga	price	*bayar*	to pay
mahal	expensive	*murah*	cheap
lagi	again, more	*uang*	money
cukup	enough	*sekarang*	now
terlalu	too	*semua*	all
banyak	much, many	*sedikit*	few, little
lebih	greater, more	*kurang*	fewer, less
habis	gone, finished	*masih*	still, remain
jauh	far	*dekat*	near
hari	day	*malam*	night
pagi	morning	*siang*	midday
hotel	hotel	*mobil*	car
bagus	good	*jelek*	bad
besar	big	*kecil*	small
sudah	already	*belum*	not yet

Questions

As in English, interrogative words and phrases are used to form questions:

Apa?	What?
Apa ini?	What is this?
Siapa?	Who?
Kalau?	If? What about?
Kapan?	When?
Kenapa?	Why? What did you say?
Mana?	Where?
Bagaimana?	How?
Yang mana?	Which one?
Di mana?	Where is it?
Ke mana?	To where?
Dari mana?	From where?

The Komodo dragon, world's largest lizard.

Kapan datang di sini? When did you arrive here?
(lit: When-arrive-at-here?)

Tuan/Nyonya dari mana? Where are you from?
(lit: Sir/Madam-from-where?)

Siapa nama ibu/bapak? What is your (his, her) name?
(lit: Who-name-Mr./Mrs.?)

Bagaimana saya bisa...? How can I...?
(lit: How-I-can-...?)

Kenapa tidak bisa...? Why can't I...?
(lit: Why-not-can-...?)

Mau ke mana? Where are you going?
(lit: Want-to-where?)

Kalau ini bagaimana? What about this one?
(lit: If-this-how?)

Di mana...? Where is...?
(lit: At-where-...?)

Di mana kamar kecil/W.C.? Where is the restroom/W.C.?
(lit: At-where-small room/W.C.?)

Note: *W.C.* is pronounced "way-say": *pria* = men's;
wanita = ladies'

The above question words do not always have to be used
in order to ask a question. The fact that you are posing a
question can also be clear from the context or by using a
rising intonation at the end of the sentence. To be even
more clear, you may also introduce the question with
apakah, which roughly translates as "Is it the case that...?"

Apakah masih ada...? Do you still have any...?
(lit: Whether-still-have...?)

Apakah di sini ada...? Do you have any...here?
(lit: Whether-at here-have...?)

Simple Phrases

The following are simple sentences that will be used often, and should be memorized.

Ada...? Is there any...? Do you have any? Are there any...?
(lit: Have...?)

Saya mau... I would like... I intend to...
(lit: I-want...)

Tidak mau! I don't want to! I don't want any!

Saya mau pergi ke... I want to go to...
(lit: I-want-go-to-...)

Saya mau minum... I would like to drink some...
(lit: I-want-drink-...)

Saya mau makan... I would like to eat some...
(lit: I-want-eat-...)

Saya mau beli ini/itu... I want to buy this/that...
(lit: I-want-buy-this/that.)

Berapa harganya? How much does it cost?
(lit: How much-its price?)   What is the price?

Saya mau bayar. I want to pay.
(lit: I-want-pay.)

Terlalu mahal! Too expensive!

Tidak bisa! This/That is not possible!

When you interrupt or pass by someone, you should say:

Permisi! Excuse me!

When an actual apology is required, use:

Ma'af! or ***Sorry!*** I'm sorry!

Ma'af, saya tidak mengerti. I'm sorry, I don't (or
(lit: Sorry, I-not-understand.)   didn't) understand.

Bapak Peter mau makan sekarang? Do you want to
(lit: Mr. Peter-want-eat-now?)   eat now, Mr. Peter?

Ibu Susan mau pergi sekarang? Do you want to go
(lit: Mrs. Susan-want-go-now?)   now, Mrs. Susan?

Note: You may find it strange that Indonesians refer to
you in English as "Mr. Peter" and "Mrs. Susan" (especially if you are not married!), but this is simply a trans-
lation of the Indonesian forms of address **bapak + first
name** and **ibu + first name** described above.

Requests

Requests may be made in a number of different ways.
Note that the English word "please" has no direct equivalent in Indonesian, and is translated differently depending upon the circumstances and the type of request that
is being made. These various translations of "please"
should not be confused.

Tolong literally means "to help." It is used to politely introduce a request when you are asking someone to do
something for you.

Tolong panggil taksi. Please (help me) summon a taxi.
(lit: Help-call-taxi.)

Boleh means "to permit" and is used in the sense of
"May I please..." when asking politely to see or do something, for example in a shop.

Boleh saya lihat ini? May I please see this?
(lit: May-I-see-this?)

Boleh saya bicara dengan...? May I please speak with...?
(lit: May-I-speak-with...?)

Boleh saya lihat itu? May I please look at that?
(lit: May-I-see-that?)

Minta means "to request" and is a polite way of asking for things like food or drink in a restaurant. Note that the use of *saya* (meaning "I") beforehand is optional.

Minta air minum.   [I] would please like some
(lit: Ask-water-to drink.)   drinking water.

Saya minta nasi goreng.   I would please like some
(lit: I-ask-fried rice.)   fried rice.

Saya pesan is another way of prefacing a request, and means simply "I wish to order some…"

Saya pesan nasi goreng.   I wish to order some fried
(lit: I-order-fried rice.)   rice.

Kasih means "to give," and is a somewhat more direct and less polite way of ordering something. It is also used after *tolong* to politely request a specific item or specific quantity of something.

Kasih air minum.   Give me some drinking
(lit: Give-water-to drink.)   water.

Tolong kasih itu.   Please give me that one.
(lit: Help-give-that.)

Tolong kasih dua.   Please give me two [of them].
(lit: Help-give-two.)

Coba means "to try (on)" and is also used with verbs such as *lihat* ("to see") in the sense of "Please may I see…" when asking to look at something in a shop window or a display case, for example:

Coba lihat itu.   Please let me have a look
(lit: Try-see-that.)   at that.

Silakan means "Please go ahead!" or "Please be my guest!" and is used by a host to invite his or her guests to do something, or as a response to a request for permission to do something. It is, for example, polite to wait for an Indonesian host or hostess to say *Silakan!* before partaking of drinks or snacks that have been placed before you. (Please note that *silakan* is never used in the sense of "please" when requesting something.)

Silakan masuk!	Please come in!
Silakan duduk!	Please sit down!
Silakan minum!	Please drink!
Silakan makan!	Please eat!
Boleh saya masuk? ***Silakan!***	May I come in? Please do!

Terima kasih is used to say "thank you." It literally means "to receive love"; it also is used to mean "no thank you" when refusing something being offered. Indonesians tend to use it much less often than it is used in English.

Sama-sama! ("same-same") or ***Kembali!*** ("return") are the normal responses to ***terimah kasih***, both meaning "You're welcome."

The famous Tanah Lot temple complex in Bali, silhouetted at sunset.

Numbers

Ordinal Numbers

se- prefix indicating one

puluh ten, multiples of ten		**ribu** thousand	
belas teen		**juta** million	
ratus hundred		**milyar** billion	

nol, kosong zero			
satu one		**sebelas** eleven	
dua two		**dua belas** twelve	
tiga three		**tiga belas** thirteen	
empat four		**empat belas** fourteen	
lima five		**lima belas** fifteen	
enam six		**enam belas** sixteen	
tujuh seven		**tujuh belas** seventeen	
delapan eight		**delapan belas** eighteen	
sembilan nine		**sembilan belas** nineteen	
sepuluh ten			

dua puluh twenty		**dua puluh satu** twenty-one	
tiga puluh thirty		**dua puluh dua** twenty-two	
empat puluh forty		**dua puluh tiga** twenty-three	
lima puluh fifty		**dua puluh empat** twenty-four	
enam puluh sixty		**dua puluh lima** twenty-five	
tujuh puluh seventy		**dua puluh enam** twenty-six	
delapan puluh eighty		**dua puluh tujuh** twenty-seven	
sembilan puluh ninety		etc.	

seratus	one hundred
dua ratus	two hundred
tiga ratus	three hundred
	etc.
seratus lima belas	one hundred fifteen
dua ratus sembilan puluh	two hundred ninety
tujuh ratus tiga puluh enam	seven hundred thirty-six
seribu	one thousand
dua ribu	two thousand
tiga ribu	three thousand
	etc.
seribu lima ratus	one thousand five hundred
sembilan ribu sebelas	nine thousand eleven
delapan ratus ribu	eight hundred thousand

Cardinal numbers

Cardinal numbers are formed by attaching the prefix *ke-* to any ordinal number. The word *yang* meaning "the one which is" may also be added when no noun is mentioned, to convey the sense of "the first one" (literally: "the one which is first"), "the second one" and so forth.

(yang) pertama	(the) first
(yang) kedua	(the) second
(yang) ketiga	(the) third
(yang) keempat	(the) fourth
(yang) kelima	(the) fifth
	etc.
(yang) terakhir	(the) last

Fractions

setengah, separoh	one half
satu per tiga, sepertiga	one third
satu per empat, seperempat	one fourth
tiga per empat	three fourths
dua per lima	two fifths
dua setengah	two and a half

Money

Note: The Indonesian unit of currency is the Rupiah, abbreviated as Rp.

Harga ini berapa, bu? What is the price of this, Bu?

Enam ratus lima puluh rupiah. Rp650.

Tiga ribu tujuh ratus lima puluh rupiah. Rp3.750.

Delapan puluh lima ribu lima ratus rupiah. Rp85.500.

Seratus lima puluh lima ribu rupiah. Rp155.000.

Tau-tau figurines in Tana Toraja, Sulawesi, represent ancestors' souls.

Etiquette and Body Language

In Indonesia, body language is as much a part of effective communication as speech. By it you may either quickly offend or put someone at ease.

Indonesians may tolerate shorts and T-shirts in tourist shops, hotels and at the beach, but not in their homes or places of worship. It is customary to wear long pants and a shirt with a collar for men, long pants or a skirt below the knees and a blouse with sleeves for women, when going out in public. Sarongs, short pants and T-shirts are only worn around the house. In Bali, a colored sash must be worn tied around the waist when entering a temple.

Avoid using the left hand. Indonesians use their right hand to eat with and their left hand to do their business!

Point with the thumb, never with the index finger. Raise or nod you head instead of pointing at people.

It is not polite to put your hands on your hips, or to cross your arms in front of you when speaking to someone.

Footwear should be taken off (*ditanggal*) when visiting an Indonesian home. Slippers or sandals are acceptable at all but the most formal of occasions.

Avoid exposing the sole of your foot at someone.

Avoid touching the head or slapping someone on the back.

Indonesians are not accustomed to public displays of affection (hugging and kissing).

Beckon someone with the hand by waving with fingers together and the palm facing downwards.

Javanese will often stoop or bend over slightly when passing you. This is based on the traditional custom in the Javanese *kraton* or palace, where the level of one's head is equated with one's social status. Servants were formerly expected to walk with their legs squat, crab-like.

Indonesians bathe at least twice daily, before breakfast and supper, and may find it very strange if you do not do the same! A common greeting in the evening is *Sudah mandi belum?* ("Have you had your bath yet?") Nothing in particular is meant by this, it is simply another way of saying "Hello!"

When visiting an Indonesian home, it is normal to greet the head of the household first. Greetings can be somewhat long and complicated. It is polite to shake hands, and to nod the head and state one's name while doing so. You will be expected to meet all adults in the house, and to go through a litany of "Small Talk" questions and answers (see Part Three below).

Wait for the signal *Silakan!* before entering, sitting, eating or drinking. Never completely finish food or drink presented to you, as to do so is to request more. Wait for your host or hostess to offer.

When you leave, say goodbye to all adults in the house,

A decorated fishing boat plies the waters off the island of Madura.

shake hands again and tell them where you are going and why you must leave so soon. Often you will be asked to stay longer, eat, bathe, take a nap, or spend the night when you were not expecting to! These elaborate rituals reinforce the atmosphere of congeniality in Indonesian society and such invitations are not to be taken seriously unless they are repeated several times. Always decline an invitation gracefully the first time, as the person making it is perhaps just being polite and doesn't really expect you to accept.

Outbursts and public displays of emotion or displeasure are to be avoided at all costs.

A dancer in the lavish Ramayana ballet of Yogyakarta, Central Java.

Grammar

Verbs

The verb is the heart of the Indonesian sentence. The following is a list of verbs that are commonly used in everyday speech. We suggest you memorize them, since they will come up again and again.

ada to be, have, exist	**bicara** to speak
mau to want (= will)	**perlu** to need
bisa to be able to (= can)	**tahu** to know
suka to like	**punya** to own

boleh to be permitted, allowed to (= may)

dapat to get, reach, attain

harus to be necessary (= must)

jadi to become, happen

Common verbs of motion (intransitive)

datang to come, arrive	**duduk** to sit
ikut to accompany, go along	**jalan** to walk, travel
keluar to go out, exit	**masuk** to go in, enter
pergi to go	**berhenti** to stop
pulang to go back [home]	**kembali** return

turun to come down, get off (a bus, etc.)

mulai to begin	**lari** to run, flee

Common verbs of action (transitive)

ambil to take, get	*bawa* to carry
beli to buy	*cari* to look for, seek
dengar to hear	*kasih* to give
lihat to see	*naik* to ride, go up, climb up
pakai to use, wear	*sewa* to rent
taruh to put, place	*terima* to receive

The verb "to be"

Note that the English verb "to be" is rarely translated in Indonesian. Sentences of the sort **X is Y** in English are translated by simply juxtaposing **X** with **Y**. The verb "to be" is then understood.

Saya orang Amerika. I [am] an American.

Hotel itu mahal. That hotel [is] expensive.

Restoran ini bagus. This restaurant [is] good.

A Sundanese couple at their wedding ceremony, in West Java.

A*dalah* may sometimes be used to join two nouns in the sense of **X is Y** although this is usually optional. (***Adalah*** cannot be used in this way, however, to join a noun with an adjective.)

Saya adalah orang Inggris. I *am* a Britisher.

Dia adalah orang yang cerdik. He *is* a clever person.

Word order

The standard or basic word order of Indonesian sentences is the same as in English, namely: **subject + verb + object + complement**.

Saya perlu taksi. I need a taxi.

Saya perlu taksi besok pagi.
I need a taxi tomorrow morning.

Kita cari hotel. We are looking for a hotel.

Saya mau sewa kamar. I want to rent a room.

John datang kemarin. John arrived yesterday.

Dia berangkat ke Bali besok.
He will leave for Bali tomorrow.

There is one very basic difference, however. In Indonesian, the most important noun or "topic" of the sentence is normally placed first. If the topic of the sentence happens to be the object of the verb, then this will be placed first and the "passive form" of the verb with *di-* will often be used (see below).

Bapak mau ke mana? Where is Bapak going?
(lit: Father-want-to-where?)

Buku itu ditaruh di sana. Put the book over there.
(lit: Book-that-put-at-there.)

Buah ini dimakan. This fruit is to be eaten. (i.e. "Go
(lit: Fruit-this-to be eaten.)   ahead and eat this fruit!")

Very often the subject of a sentence is omitted, as it is clear from the context.

Mau pergi? Do [*you*] want to go?

Ada kamar? Do [*you*] have any rooms?

Minta air minum. [*I*] would like some drinking water.

Boleh lihat? May [*I*] see?

Verb forms

While verbs are not conjugated for person and number as in most European languages, there are a number of verbal prefixes and suffixes that alter or reinforce the meaning of a verb in various ways. The most common is the "active" prefix *me-*. This and other affixes are commonly omitted in everyday conversation, however. For further information on these verbal affixes, see Appendix A.

Saya mau melihat Borobudur. I want to see Borobudur.

Saya mau lihat Borobudur. (same)

The passive form *di-*

The passive form of a transitive verb is formed with the prefix *di-*. Note that the passive form often implies an imperative or a necessity.

Sepatu ini boleh dicoba. The shoes may be tried on.
                 (i.e. "You may try on the shoes.")

Dicoba dulu! Try it/them [on] first!

Nasi ini dimasak. This rice is to be cooked.
                 (i.e. "Cook this rice!")

Tense

Verbs do not change their form to indicate tense, the same form of the verb is used to speak of the past, present and future. Usually it is clear from the context which is intended. To be more specific, auxiliary verbs and words indicating a specific time reference may be added, just as in English.

Saya makan. I eat. I am eating.

Saya **sudah** *makan.* I have *already* eaten.

Saya makan **tadi.** I ate *just now.*

Saya **akan** *makan.* I *will* eat.

Saya makan **nanti.** I will eat *later.*

Present tense

If no auxiliary verb or specific time reference is used, it is generally assumed that one is speaking about the present.

Sekarang ("now") is used to emphasize the fact that one is speaking about the present.

Kita pergi **sekarang.** We are leaving *now.*

Saya mau makan **sekarang.** I want to eat *now.*

Sedang is another auxiliary used in the sense of "to be in the middle of" doing something:

Saya **sedang** *makan.* I am *in the middle of* eating.

Kita **sedang** *bicara.* We are *in the middle of* speaking.

Future tense

Akan ("shall, will") is an auxiliary verb used to express the future.

> *Tahun depan saya* **akan** *kembali ke Indonesia lagi.*
> Next year I *will* return to Indonesia again.

Mau ("to want to") is often used as an auxiliary verb to signify the near future, just as in English. It is then followed by the main verb. In this case it often has the sense of "to intend to, will" do something.

> *Besok saya* **mau** *pergi ke candi Borobudur.*
> Tomorrow I *want to* [intend to, will] go to the Borobudur temple.

Nanti ("later") is also used as a specific time reference indicating future tense, often after **mau + verb**:

> *Saya pergi* **nanti.** I will go *later.*

> *Saya mau pergi* **nanti.** I intend to go *later.*

Women in Bali carrying offerings to the temple.

Past tense

Sudah ("already") is used in Indonesian to indicate most forms of the past tense in English. It is placed before the verb, and is often not translated in English.

Dia sudah **pergi?** Has he gone *already?*

Ya, dia sudah **pergi.** Yes, he has gone *already.*

Saya sudah belajar bahasa Indonesia satu bulan.
I have [already] been studying Indonesian one month.

Kemarin ("yesterday") and **tadi** ("just now, earlier") are specific time references used to indicate the past.

Kemarin *saya bicara dengan dia.*
I spoke with him/her *yesterday.*

Saya datang tadi. I arrived *just now.*

Past tense with *waktu* ("the time when")

Waktu ("time" or "the time when") is another time reference used to indicate actions which occurred in the past. Followed by *itu* ("that") it means "by that time" or "at that time" and indicates what in English would be a pluperfect tense.

Waktu *dia datang, kita sedang makan.*
When (at the time) he arrived, we were eating.

Waktu itu *saya baru pulang.*
At that time, I had just come home.

Waktu may also be combined with *sudah* to indicate the pluperfect tense:

Waktu *dia datang, kita* sudah *makan.*
When he arrived, we had *already* eaten.

Waktu itu *saya sudah pergi.*
By that time I had already gone.

Past tense with *pernah* ("to have ever")

Pernah is an auxiliary verb meaning "to have been" or "to have ever" done something. When placed before the main verb, like *sudah*, it expresses the past tense, but is not usually translated in English. It is commonly used together with *sudah* to emphasize past action.

> **Saya** pernah *lihat itu.*   I have seen that.

> **Saya** sudah pernah *lihat itu.*   I have seen that before.

Pernah is often used on its own, without another verb.

> **Anda** pernah *ke sana?* Have you *ever* been there *before*?

> **Saya** pernah *ke sana.*   I have been there *before.*

When used negatively with *tidak* or *belum*, *pernah* has the sense of "never" or "not yet":

> **Saya** tidak pernah *makan daging.*   I *never* eat meat.

> **Saya** belum pernah *ke sana.*   I have *not yet* been there.

Cakalele dancer in Manado with Portuguese-style helmet.

Negation

Tidak, meaning not, is the most common negative word, used to negate verbs and adjectives. Spoken contracted forms of *tidak* are **ndak** and **nggak**.

Hotel ini tidak *bagus.* This hotel is *not* good.

Dia tidak *pergi.* He/she is *not* going.

Kenapa John nggak *datang?* Why *didn't* John arrive?

Whenever possible, however, Indonesians prefer to use **kurang** ("less") or **belum** ("not yet") instead of *tidak* because the latter seems to carry a sense of "finality" or to be too "strong." *Kurang* in this sense may be translated "not really" or "not very":

Hotel ini kurang *baik.* This hotel is *not very* good.

Saya kurang *senang itu.* I *don't really* like it.

Dia kurang *mengerti.* He *doesn't really* understand.

Kenapa Joe belum *datang?* Why *hasn't* Joe arrived *yet?*

Belum ("not yet") is also more commonly used than *tidak,* as a response to a question involving time or action.

Dia sudah pergi? Belum. Has he gone? *Not yet.*

Anda sudah pernah ke Bali? Belum.
Have you ever been to Bali? *Not yet.*

Bukan is used to negate nouns rather than *tidak*:

Bukan *ini, itu.* *Not* this (one), that (one).

Itu bukan *lukisan tapi batik.*
That is *not* a painting but a batik.

Itu bukan *masalah saya.* That is *not* my problem.

Jangan! ("Don't!") is used to express negative imperatives instead of *tidak.*

Jangan *pergi!* *Don't* go!

Jangan *mau!* *Don't* want! (lit: *Don't* accept it!)

Nouns

anak child	*orang* person, human being
buku book	*nama* name
makanan food	*minuman* drink
mata eye	*hari* day
mobil car	*bis* bus
kamar room	*rumah* house, home
kursi chair, seat	*meja* table
tempat place, seat	*kota* town, city
jalan street, road	*kunci* key
teman friend	*air* water
suami husband	*isteri* wife
nasi rice (cooked)	*gelas* glass
gunung mountain	*pantai* beach
karcis ticket	*barang* goods, item
hal matter	*masalah* problem
muka face	*belakang* back
bahasa language	*negara* country
sendok spoon	*garpu* fork
piring plate	*hotel* hotel

Articles

Unlike English, Indonesian does not use any articles (a, an, the) before nouns:

Saya akan naik bis ke Bali.
I will take *the* bus to Bali.

Kita cari hotel yang murah.
We are looking for *a* cheap hotel.

Kita mau sewa kamar. We want to rent *a* room.

Ada kunci? Do you have *the* key?

The sense of the English definite article ("the") can often be conveyed, however, by the possessive suffix *-nya* (literally: "his, hers, its, yours") or by the demonstrative pronouns *ini* and *itu* ("this" and "that"):

Orangnya tinggi. *The* person [is] tall.

Bis itu di mana? Where is *the* [that] bus?

Batik ini mahal. *The* [this] batik is expensive.

Topeng dancers from Cirebon, West Java, pose with their masks.

Grammar

Plural forms

Singular or plural forms of nouns are not normally distinguished, and the same form is used for both. Singular or plural are indicated instead by the context, or through the use of other words such as "all," "many," etc.

Semua *orang senang.* *All* the people were pleased.

Banyak *turis datang.* *Many* tourists arrived.

Reduplicating a noun may emphasize that it is plural:

> ***anak-anak*** (also written ***anak2***) children

> ***buku-buku*** books

However, reduplication really carries the meaning "a variety of." It is also used to create new words with very different meanings from the simple forms. It is best therefore to avoid reduplication to indicate the plural unless you know what you are saying.

> ***mata*** eye   ***mata-mata*** spy

> ***semata-mata*** only, exclusively

A Madurese man and his festively-attired racing bulls.

Para indicates plural for persons:

para *penumpang* passengers

para *penonton* viewers

Note: More information concerning noun formation using prefixes and suffixes is given at the back of this book.

Classifier words

A number cannot be placed before many Indonesian nouns without the use of certain "classifier words" between the number and the noun. This is analagous to the use of words in English such as "two *pieces* of cake" or "three *sheets* of paper," etc. Some of the more common classifiers are listed below.

batang (lit: "trunk") used for cigarettes, trees, etc.

biji (lit: "seed") used for small objects

buah (lit: "fruit") used for larger and abstract things

ekor (lit: "tail") used for animals

helai (lit: "sheet") used for paper

lembar (lit: "sheet") used for paper, wood, etc.

orang (lit: "person") used for people

pasang (lit: "pair") used for socks, trousers, etc.

potong (lit: "cut") used for bread, cloth, etc.

pucuk (lit: "sprout") used for letters

tusuk (lit: "stick") used for satay

tiga orang *docter* three doctors

dua ekor *ayam* two chickens

sepuluh batang *rokok* ten cigarettes

dua potong *roti* two slices of bread

lima pucuk *surat* three letters

Adjectives

Some common adjectives are listed below together with their opposites.

baru new	**lama** old (of things)
muda young	**tua** old (of persons)
baik, bagus good	**jelek** bad, ugly
besar big	**kecil** small
mahal expensive	**murah** cheap
tinggi tall, high (height)	**pendek** short
panjang long (length)	**lebar** wide (width)
pelan slow	**cepat** fast
penuh full	**kosong** empty
sama the same	**lain** different
ringan light	**berat** heavy
mudah, gampang easy	**susah, sukar** difficult

Noun modifiers such as adjectives and possessives always follow the word being modified, with the relative pronoun *yang* (meaning "[the one] which") sometimes intervening (see below):

mobil baru new car

mobil yang baru the new car (lit: "the car which is new")

gadis (yang) muda (the) young girl

orang (yang) baik (the) good person

gedung (yang) tinggi (the) high building

buku saya my book

rumah bapak your house (lit: "father's house")

anak dia or **anaknya** his/their child (*-nya = dia*)

negeri kita our country

Comparatives and superlatives

baik	*lebih baik*	*paling baik*
good	better	best
cepat	*lebih cepat*	*paling cepat*
fast	faster	fastest
tinggi	*lebih tinggi*	*paling tinggi*
tall	taller	tallest

Lebih ("more") and **kurang** ("less") are used with adjectives to form comparatives. If the thing being compared to is mentioned, this follows the word *daripada* ("than") or *dibandingkan* ("compared to").

Dia lebih **pintar.**
He/she is cleverer.

Dia lebih **pintar** daripada **saya.**
He/she is cleverer than I.

Made lebih **muda** daripada **Peter.**
Made is younger than Peter.

A retinue of palace guards at the kraton in Yogyakarta, Central Java.

Hotel ini lebih *baik* daripada *itu*.
This hotel is better than that one.

Dia lebih *tinggi* daripada *saya*.
She/he is taller than I am.

Bis ini lebih *cepat* daripada *itu*.
This bus is faster than that one.

Ini kurang *baik*.
This one is not as good.

Ini kurang *baik* dibandingkan *itu*.
This [one] is not as good as that [one].

Amat kurang *tinggi* dibandingkan *John*.
Amat is not as tall as John. (lit: "less tall compared to John")

Note: *Daripada* is often shortened to *dari*.

Batik ini lebih mahal dari *itu*.
This batik is more expensive than that one.

Paling ("the most") is used to form the superlatives "most, -est." Another way is to add the prefix *ter-*.

> paling *baik*, ter*baik* the best

> paling *mahal*, ter*mahal* the most expensive

> paling *baru*, ter*baru* the newest

Note: The reduplicated form ***paling-paling*** means "at most":

Ke Semarang paling-paling *perlu dua jam*.
To (get to) Semarang requires *at most* two hours.

Equality

Equality is expressed by the prefix **se-** ("the same as") plus an adjective.

Dia setinggi saya. He is *the same* height *as* I.

The construction **-nya sama** after a noun also expresses equality.

Harganya sama. The prices are *the same.*

Umurnya sama. (Our, Their) ages are *the same.*

Tingginya sama. (Our, Their) heights are *the same.*

Warnanya sama. The colors are *the same.*

Possessives

Like adjectives, possesives follow the noun they modify:

Ini buku Eric. This is Eric*'s* book.

Ini rumah saya. This is *my* house.

Sudah sampai ke hotel Bapak.
   We have reached *your* (Bapak's) hotel.

Punya "to own, belong to" is a transitive verb that can be used to emphasize the relation of possession and make it clearer who is owning what. Note that the principle topic of the sentence always comes first.

Ini punya saya. This belongs to me.

Mobil itu punya siapa? Who owns that car?

Nyoman punya tiga isteri. Nyoman has three wives.

Orang itu tidak punya uang. That person has no money.

The abbreviated forms of personal pronouns **-ku** "my" for *aku* and **-mu** "your" for *kamu* may be suffixed to nouns, but should only be used to address persons one is intimately aquainted with or children.

Berapa umurmu? What is *your* age?

Itu harapanku. That is *my* hope.

The suffix -nya

Adding the suffix **-nya** to a noun is equivalent to placing the third person pronouns **dia** or **mereka** immediately after a noun to express possession. It therefore means **his**, **her**, **its** or **their** (sometimes also **your**).

Ini buku John. This is John's book.

Ini buku dia. This is *his* (her, their) book.

Ini bukunya. This is *his* (her, their) book.

This suffix **-nya** is also used when a possessive would be unnecessary in English, in which case it takes the sense of the English definite pronoun **the**:

Mobilnya di sana. *The* car is over there.

Hotelnya di mana? Where is *the* hotel?

Village girls in the Mamasa area of South Sulawesi.

Adverbs

Like adjectives, most adverbs follow the words they modify.

begini, begitu thus, so	**juga** also, too
dulu before, first	**saja** only, just
sekali very (also "once"; *dua kali* = "twice")	

Dia pergi juga. He will go *also*.

Saya berangkat dulu. I am leaving *first*.

Minta air putih saja. I would like drinking water *only*.

Makanan ini enak sekali. This food is *very* tasty.

However, the following commonly used adverbs precede the verbs they modify:

belum not yet	**cuma** merely
hampir almost	**hanya** only
kira-kira approximately	**masih** still
sangat very, extremely	**sudah** already
terlalu too (excessive)	

Saya masih *makan*.
I am *still* eating.

Kita hampir *sampai di Solo*.
We have *almost* arrived at Solo.

Hal ini sangat *penting*.
This matter is *extremely* important.

Saya hanya *mau beli tiga buah*.
I *only* want to buy three pieces.

Barang ini terlalu *mahal*!
This item is *too* expensive!

Prepositions

Di "in," *dari* "from," and *ke* "to, toward" are the most common prepositions.

> *Dia ada* di *rumah sekarang.* He/she is *in* the house now.

> *Saya lari* dari *sana.* I ran *from* there.

> *Saya mau* ke *Bandung.* I want to go *to* Bandung.

> *Saya mau pergi* ke *Bali.* I would like to go *to* Bali.

Di is combined with the following words to form a number of common phrases indicating location:

di sini here	*di sana, di situ* there
di dalam inside	*di luar* outside
di bawah below, downstairs	*di atas* above, upstairs
di depan in front of	*di belakang* behind
di muka in front of	*di sebelah* next (door) to
di seberang across (the street) from	

Imperatives

To form the imperative, the suffix *-lah* is added to the verb:

> *Pergilah!* Go!　　　　　*Makanlah!* Eat!

Mari, mari kita or (more colloquially) *ayo* are used as hortatives ("come let us"):

Mari *makan*.
　　Come, let's eat.

Mari kita *berangkat sekarang*.
　　Come, let's depart now.

Ayo *pulang*, ayo.
　　Come on, let's go home.

Note: The word *ayo* is very commonly used, just as in English we would say "C'mon" or "Let's go!"

The relative pronoun *yang*

Yang is an all-purpose relative pronoun meaning "the one which," "the one who," "that which." It is most often used in the construction:

> *[noun]* + yang + *[adjective]*
>   the [noun] *which is* [adjective]

If a noun is not specified, it simply means "*the* [adjective] *one*."

> *Saya cari batik* yang *besar.*
>   I am looking for a large batik. (lit: "a batik which is large")

> *Saya cari hotel* yang *murah.*
>   I am looking for a cheap hotel. (lit: "a hotel which is cheap")

> **Yang** *hitam?* The black one?

> *Bukan,* yang *merah.* No, the red one.

Yang is also used in certain set phrases like *Yang mana?* ("Which one?"), *yang ini* ("this one") and *yang itu* ("that one"):

> *Ibu mau* yang mana?
>   *Which one* would you ("mother") like?

> **Yang ini?** *This one?*

> *Bukan,* yang itu.   No, *that one.*

Yang is also used to introduce subordinate clauses, just like the English word "which."

> *Kain batik* yang *kita beli sudah hilang.*
>   The batik cloth *which* we bought is lost.

> *Film* yang *kita lihat itu bagus sekali!*
>   That film *which* we saw was very good!

A Sundanese boy in West Java.

Small Talk

Indonesians are great talkers. They are also an instinctively inquisitive people, and will often approach you on buses or trains to strike up a conversation. As expressed in the common greetings *Mau ke mana?* and *Sudah makan belum?* they always seem to want to know where you are going, what you are doing, who you are, whether you have eaten or bathed yet, etc. Just as we automatically say "How are you?" or "How do you do?" in English when meeting someone, these greetings do not require a specific answer, but are simply another way of saying hello.

Once the greetings are over, however, visitors will frequently find themselves barraged with a series of more specific questions, including many that seem to concern very personal and intimate matters, such as family background, marital status, religious beliefs, and so forth. These will come up again and again until you can almost predict which question is coming next, and are probably quite tired of this whole "interview" process.

Try not be put off or angered by this. Understand that your "interviewers" are simply trying to be friendly, and are using such topics to make small talk, much as Westerners would discuss the weather or sports. Realize that in Indonesia such information is not considered personal at all, it is simply a part of one's identity—like your name, nationality and address. If you do not wish to answer, it is perfectly acceptable to be evasive or to joke around. Most Indonesians will never press you for an answer. On the other hand, you can use this as an opportunity to practice your Indonesian, and by turning the questions around you can also learn something about the people you meet.

The following sections will equip you with basic phrases and vocabulary to deal with these "20 questions" that you will encounter again and again when traveling in Indonesia.

Name and nationality

One of the first questions asked, following your name, will be about your nationality.

> ***Nama bapak/ibu siapa?*** or ***Siapa nama bapak/ibu?***
> What is your name?

> ***Nama saya Martin.***   ***Nama saya Jane.***
> My name is Martin.   My name is Jane.

> ***Bapak/Ibu asal dari mana?*** or ***Asal bapak/ibu dari mana?*** or ***Asalnya dari mana?***
> Where do you originate from?

> ***Saya dari Amerika.*** I am from America.
> or ***Saya orang Amerika.*** I am American.

Australi	Australian
Belanda	Dutch
Denmark	Danish
Inggeris	British
Italia	Italian
Jepang	Japanese
Jerman	German
Kanada	Canadian
Muangthai	Thai
Norwegia	Norwegian
Perancis	French
Selandia Baru	a New Zealander
Sepanyol	Spanish

Suedia	Swedish
Suis	Swiss
Tionghoa	Chinese
Yunani	Greek

Note that *Inggeris* alone or *negeri Inggeris* means the country, England (or Great Britain), *orang Inggeris* is a Britisher and *bahasa Inggeris* is the English language. Similarly, *Jerman* or *negeri Jerman* is Germany, *orang Jerman* is a German person and *bahasa Jerman* is the language. So it is with the other countries, nationalities and languages.

Age

The next thing most people want to know is your age.

umur age

berumur to be of the age, have the age...

tahun year(s)   **lahir** to be born

muda young   **tua** old

Umur bapak/ibu berapa (tahun)? How old are you?
(lit: "Your age is how many [years]?")

Umur saya empat puluh satu. I am 41.
(lit: "My age is 41.")

Saya berumur tiga puluh tahun. I am 30 years old.

Saya lahir tahun sembilan belas enam puluh satu.
    I was born in 1961.

In answering evasively, you may want to joke and say:

Saya sudah tua, mau pension.
    I am already old, ready to retire.

Saya masih muda. I am still young.

Saya masih anak. I am still a child.

Family

Next you will be asked about your family and marital status. Indonesians expect all adults over 25 to be married and all married couples to have children, and will be surprised if they find this is not the case. If you are over 25 and still single, and don't wish to pursue the matter further, you might consider just saying that you are married and have three children anyway (which is what the person asking expects you to say).

ayah, bapak father	***ibu*** mother
isteri wife	***suami*** husband
perempuan woman, female	***laki-laki*** male, man
kawin, nikah to be married	***keluarga*** family

saudara brother or sister (sibling)

adik younger sibling	***kakak*** older sibling
pacar boy or girlfriend	***teman, kawan*** friend

anak child	***orang*** person
anak perempuan daughter	***anak laki-laki*** son

cucu grandchild, grand niece or nephew

orang tua parents (lit: "old people")

Bapak/Ibu sudah kawin belum?
Are you married yet?

Sudah/Belum. Already/Not yet.

Masih terlalu muda. (I am) still too young.

Bapak/Ibu punya berapa anak?
How many children do you have?

Saya punya tiga anak. I have three children.

Satu laki-laki dan dua perempuan.
One son and two daughters.

Tuan punya berapa saudara?
How many brothers and sisters do you have?

Saya punya tiga saudara. I have three siblings.

Kakak laki-laki satu dan adik perempuan dua.
One older brother and two younger sisters.

Additional vocabulary

bayi baby ***bibi*** aunt ***cerai*** divorced

famili relatives, family ***ipar*** brother, sister-in-law

kakek grandfather, grand uncle

keponakan niece or nephew

menantu son/daughter-in-law

mertua father/mother-in-law

nenek grandmother, grand aunt

paman uncle ***saudara sepupu*** cousin

Javanese men sporting the *peci* or Islamic cap.

Occupation

Next will be questions concerning your job or profession. Most educated Indonesians carry a business card. They may offer you one and ask for yours. After even a brief conversation, many people will want to have your address. If you will be traveling for very long in Indonesia, it is a good idea to have some cards printed up. This can be done cheaply and quickly in any town, and saves you from having to write out your name and address.

bekerja to work	*pension* retired
perusahaan company	*belajar* to study
kartu card	*kartu nama* name card

Bapak/Ibu bekerja di mana? Where do you work?

Saya bekerja di perusahan... I work at company...

Saya bekerja di kantor. I work in an office.

Saya belajar di universitas.
I am studying at a university.

Saya terkena pengangguran. I am unemployed.

Ada kartu nama? Do you have a name card?

Boleh saya minta satu? May I have one?

Ma'af, tidak ada. I'm sorry I don't have one.

Additional vocabulary

ilmuwan/-wati scientist (m/f)

karyawan/-wati white collar worker (m/f)

mahasiswa university student.

olahragawan/-wati athlete (m/f)

wartawan/-wati journalist (m/f)

dosen university lecturer

manajer manager

pedagang businessman

pejabat civil servant

pelaut sailor

sekretaris secretary

guru teacher

misi missionary

pabrik factory

pengarang writer

pendeta minister

seniman artist

Religion

It is common for Indonesians to ask about your religion. For most people in Indonesia, religion is not so much a question of personal beliefs as it is a reflection of one's ethnic or cultural identity. Indonesia recognizes only five official religions: Buddhism, Hinduism, Islam, Catholicism and Protestantism, and Indonesians will expect most Westerners to be either Protestants or Catholics. Atheism is not officially recognized, and many Indonesians will not know what this means. To them, it is like not having a name or a nationality. When in doubt, just say that you are *Kristen* or *Katolik*.

agama religion

gereja church

anggota member

masuk to enter, convert

Bapak/Ibu agama apa? What religion are you?

Saya orang Hindu. I am Hindu.

Banyak orang Bali begitu. So are many Balinese.

Saya orang Islam. I am a Muslim.

Katolik Catholic

Kristen, Protestan Protestant

Budha Buddhist

Yahudi Jewish

Note: As a result of Dutch influence, Indonesians make a clear distinction between Protestants and Catholics, and have no general term to express "Christian." To say that one is *Kristen* in Indonesian means specifically that one is Protestant. Note also that in certain areas of Indonesia, where Islam is particularly strong, it may not be a good idea to say that you are Jewish, although in most places this will not create any problems.

Weather

The weather in Indonesia is hot and humid all year around, so there is not much to talk about. One thing that people do often talk about, however, are the rains and great floods or *banjir* that periodically inundate cities and towns along the coasts during the rainy season. People may also ask you how the weather is back home.

In the southernmost chain of islands (Java, Bali and Nusa Tenggara to the east), there are two seasons: a rainy season (from about November to April) and a dry one (May to October). On the other islands, closer to the equator, the rainfall is more evenly spread throughout the year, though certain months have more rain than others.

banjir flood, flooding	**hujan** rain, to be raining
derajat degrees	**cuaca** weather
matahari sun	**salju** snow
sering often, frequent[ly]	**suhu** temperature

panas hot	**dingin** cold
cerah clear	**mendung** cloudy
segar fresh, invigorating	**sejuk** cool

musim season	**iklim** climate
musim panas summer (*panas* = "hot")	
musim gugur fall (*gugur* = "to wilt")	
musim salju winter (*salju* = "snow")	

musim semi   spring (*semi* = "to sprout")

musim kemarau   dry season

musim hujan   rainy season

Cuacanya panas hari ini.   The weather is hot today.

Suhunya tiga puluh derajat.   It's 30 degrees (Celsius).

Sudah mulai hujan belum?   Have the rains begun yet?

Ya, sudah musim hujan sekarang.
Yes, it is [already] the rainy season now.

Tiap hari hujan.   It rains every day.

Tahun ini sering banjir.
This year there has been frequent flooding.

Cuaca di negeri ibu/bapak bagaimana?
How is the weather in your country?

Sekarang dingin sekali. Ada salju.
It is very cold now. There is snow.

Muslim schoolgirls along the north coast of Java.

Time

menit minute	*jam* hour, o'clock
hari day	*minggu* week
bulan month, moon	*tahun* year
hari ini today	*kemarin* yesterday
besok tomorrow	*lusa* the day after tomorrow
awal early	*terlambat* late
sebelum before	*sesudah* after
sekarang now	*dulu* earlier, first, beforehand
segera soon	*baru, baru tadi* just, just now
nanti later	*sebentar* in a moment, awhile
jarang rarely	*kadang-kadang* sometimes
sering often	*dulu* before, earlier

Women in traditional dress in Lampung, southern Sumatra.

Kapan bapak/ibu mau berangkat?
When do you want to depart?

Kita mau pergi hari ini. We want to go today.

Kita mau berangkat awal. We want to leave early.

Kereta api itu selalu terlambat!
That train is always late!

Kemarin terlambat dua jam.
Yesterday it was two hours late.

Bapak sering datang ke Indonesia?
Do you come often to Indonesia?

Jarang. Dulu pernah datang se-kali.
Rarely. I have come once before.

Kapan Ibu sampai di sini? When did you arrive here?

Baru kemarin. Just yesterday.

Kapan berangkat? When are you leaving?

Sebentar lagi. In a little while.

Telling time

Jam berapa sekarang? What time is it now?

Sekarang jam sepuluh. It is now ten o'clock.

Just as in English, there are several ways of telling the
time in Indonesian. One can say "a quarter to nine" or
"eight forty-five" or "forty-five minutes past eight."

Jam dua belas seperempat. 12:15

Jam dua belas lewat seperempat. 12:15

Jam dua belas lewat lima belas (menit). 12:15

Note that Indonesians follow the Dutch (and old English) system in telling time, in which the half hour is normally counted before, not after the hour of day:

> *Jam setengah sebelas.* Half eleven (i.e. 10:30).

To express minutes after the hour, the words *lewat* or *lebih* meaning "past" may be used, although these are optional.

> *Jam dua lewat empat puluh lima menit.* 2:45
> *Jam lima lebih dua puluh menit.* 5:20

The use of *menit* is also optional, as it is easily understood from the context.

> *Jam empat kurang sepuluh (menit).* 3:50

To express minutes before the hour, the word *kurang* "less" must be used.

> *Jam tiga kurang seperempat.* 2:45

Fractions are used just as in English.

Note: If a number precedes the word *jam*, it signifies a number of hours; if it follows, it signifies the time of day (= o'clock).

> *dua jam* two hours   *jam dua* two o'clock

> *Dari Denpasar ke Ubud berapa jam?*
> How many hours [does it take] to go from Denpasar to Ubud?

> *Satu jam.* One hour.

> *Berapa jam ke Jakarta?* How many hours to Jakarta?
> *Tiga jam setengah.* Three and a half hours.

Periods of the day

In English we break the day into **morning**, **noon**, **afternoon**, **evening** and **night**. Indonesians break up the day a bit differently (the following are approximate times).

> *pagi-pagi* early morning (5 to 7 am)
>
> *pagi* morning (7 to 11 am)
>
> *siang* midday (11 am to 3 pm)
>
> *sore* late afternoon to dusk (3 to 7 pm)
>
> *malam* night (7 to 10 pm)
>
> *malam-malam* late night (10-12 pm)
>
> *tengah malam* midnight to sunrise

Note that these periods of the day are used not only in greetings with *selamat* (see Part One: Greetings) but also in place of our am or pm in telling time.

> *jam sembilan pagi* 9 am
>
> *jam sembilan malam* 9 pm
>
> *jam dua siang* 2 pm
>
> *jam lima sore* 5 pm
>
> *jam lima pagi* 5 am

Days of the week

hari day	*(hari)* **Minggu** Sunday
(hari) **Senin** Monday	*(hari)* **Selasa** Tuesday
(hari) **Rabu** Wednesday	*(hari)* **Kamis** Thursday
(hari) **Jumat** Friday	*(hari)* **Sabtu** Saturday

Ini hari apa? What day (of the week) is it?

Ini hari Selasa. It is Tuesday.

Dates

tanggal date (of the month)

Januari	January	*Juli*	July
Pebuari	February	*Agustus*	August
Maret	March	*September*	September
April	April	*Oktober*	October
Mei	May	*Nopember*	November
Juni	June	*Desember*	December

Hari ini tanggal berapa? What is the date today?

Hari ini tanggal duabelas (bulan) Juli tahun (sembilan belas) sembilan puluh satu.
  Today is the twelfth of (the month of) July, the year 1991.

Saya mau pulang tanggal sepuluh.
  I want to go back on the tenth.

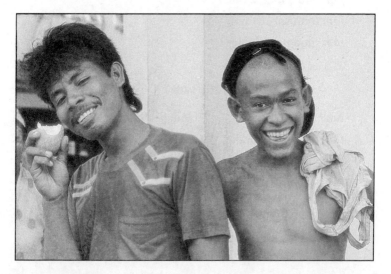

Eating fruit on the eastern Indonesian island of Ambon.

Useful words and phrases

lalu, *yang lalu* past, last,

minggu lalu, *minggu yang lalu* last week

bulan lalu, *bulan yang lalu* last month

tahun lalu, *tahun yang lalu* last year

sejak since

Sejak kapan? Since when? For how long?

Sejak tahun yang lalu. Since last year.

depan next, front

minggu depan next week

bulan depan next month

tahun depan next year

tadi a while ago

tadi pagi earlier this morning

tadi malam, *semalam* last night

tadi siang earlier today (midday)

tadi sore earlier this afternoon

nanti later

nanti siang later today (midday)

nanti sore later this afternoon

nanti malam later tonight

Note: When *malam* (night, eve) preceeds a day of the week, it indicates the night before that day (i.e. the eve of that day). When in doubt, it is best to state the date when fixing an appointment in order to remove any ambiguity.

malam Sabtu Saturday eve (= Friday night)

Sabtu malam Saturday night

A village on stilts in the Riau Islands, near Singapore.

PART FOUR

Travel

Asking directions

alamat address	*alun-alun* town square
desa village, countryside	*gedung* building
kota city, town, downtown	*rumah* house/home
pompa bensin gas station	*tempat* place

gang alleyway, lane	*jalan* street
jalan kecil side street	*jalan besar* main street
jalan raya highway, thoroughfare	*jalan tol* expressway, tollroad

lewat to pass, go by way of	*belok* to turn
kanan right	*kiri* left
terus straight	*kira-kira* approximately

Indonesians are more than willing to give you directions if they can understand what you are asking them. Note that since the place you are asking about is invariably the main topic of your question, you should always place it at or near the beginning of your sentence (not at the end, as in English). This will make your question more easily understood. It is also more polite to preface any request for directions by the phrase *Tolong tanya* (lit: "Help ask"), or *Boleh saya tanya?* ("May I ask?").

Tolong tanya. Excuse me, I wish to ask.

Hotel Savoy di mana? Where is the Hotel Savoy?

Jalan Sudirman di mana? Where is Jalan Sudirman?

Gedung Nusantara di mana?
Where is the Nusantara Building?

Ke Ubud lewat mana? How does one get to Ubud?

Ke Yogya naik apa dari sini?
How can I get to Yogya from here?
(i.e. by what means of transportation?)

Terus saja di sini, lalu belok kanan.
Straight ahead here, then turn right.

Lewat jalan ini terus, sampai jalan raya.
Follow this road straight until the highway.

Lalu belok kiri. Then turn left.

Berapa jauh (dari sini)? How far is it from here?

Kira-kira lima kilometer. About five kilometers.

Note: When asking directions, phrase your question in such a way that it cannot be answered by a simple yes or no. For example, don't say: "Is Jalan Malioboro over there?" The person being asked may not understand what you are saying and may simply respond yes or no at random. Instead, ask: "Where is Jalan Malioboro?"

Taxi directions

The following are indispensible phrases for directing taxi drivers:

Tolong panggil taksi! Please summon a taxi!

Saya mau ke... I want to go to...

Ke airport, pak. To the airport, *pak*.

Mau lewat mana? By which route?

Yang paling cepat. The fastest one.

Saya mau lewat... I want to go by way of...

Terus! or ***Lurus!*** Straight ahead!

Belok kiri/kanan. Turn left/right.

Hop! or ***Berhenti!*** Stop!

Di sini! Here!

Putar! Turn around/make a U-turn.

Mundur! Back up!

Pelan-pelan! Slowly!

Cepat! Faster!

Awas! or ***Hati-hati!*** Be careful!

Ini jurusan ke utara? Is this to the north?

           selatan? south?

           timur? east?

           barat? west?

Backpacking tourists asking directions.

Public transportation

pergi to go   *balik, kembali* to return

berangkat to depart   *datang, tiba* to arrive

batal to cancel   *tunda* to postpone

naik to ride, to go by (train, bus, etc.)

pulang to go back [home]

sampai to reach

jadwal schedule   *kantor* office

karcis ticket   *tempat duduk* seat

sopir driver   *tarip* tariff, fare, rate

setasiun (kereta api) train station

terminal (bis) bus terminal

belum not yet   *langsung* direct, non-stop

masih still, left over   *sudah* already

lambat slow   *cepat* fast

Once again, when asking a question, state the main topic first so that the person being asked knows what it is you are referring to:

Terminal bis di mana? Where is the bus terminal?

Setasiun kereta api di mana?
Where is the train station?

Ke airport berapa kilometer dari sini?
How many kilometers to the airport from here?

Taripnya berapa? What is the fare?

Ke Bali bisa naik kereta api tidak?
Can I take a train to Bali or not?

Kereta api ke Yogya berangkat jam berapa?
What time does the train to Yogya depart?

Pesawat ke Jakarta itu tiba jam berapa?
What time does that plane to Jakarta arrive?

Ke Bali hari ini ada bis lagi tidak?
Is there another bus to Bali today or not?

Masih ada tempat duduk? Are there any seats left?

Masih. Yes, there are still.

Ma'af, sudah habis. Sorry, sold out (finished) already.

Harga karcisnya berapa?
What is the price of the tickets?

Sekali jalan atau pulang pergi?
One-way or round-trip?

Sekali jalan. One way.

Taripnya lima belas ribu rupiah. The fare is Rp15.000.

Sumatran buses ready to leave the terminal.

Naik bis ke Medan berapa jam, pak?
How many hours by bus to Medan, *pak*?

Biasanya lima belas jam. Usually 15 hours.

Bis ini lambat atau cepat? Is this bus slow or fast?

Ada bis ekspres? Is there an express bus?

Berangkat jam berapa? What time does it leave?

Pakai AC ("ah-say") **tidak?**
Does it have air-conditioning or not?

Bis ke Solo itu lewat mana?
What route does that bus to Solo follow?

Sampai di Malang jam berapa?
What time does it reach Malang?

Paling cepat naik apa? What is the fastest way?

Taruh bagasi di mana?
Where do I put my baggage?

A *dokar* on the beach at Parangtritis, near Yogyakarta.

Sewa mobil ini berapa per hari?
How much does it cost to rent this car per day?

Pakai sopir tidak? Do you want it with the driver?

Tidak. Saya mau setir sendiri.
No. I want to drive myself.

Saya punya SIM internasional.
I have an international driver's license.

Modes of transportation

Saya mau naik... I want to go by...

pesawat (terbang) airplane

kapal ship

perahu boat

kereta api train

mobil car/automobile

bis (malam) (night) bus

travel door-to-door minibus service

taksi taxi

mikrolet minibus

colt (pronounced *kol*) minivan

bemo small pick-up or minivan

bajaj (pronounced *bajai*), *helicak*
three-wheeled minicar

dokar horsecart   *kuda* horse

becak pedicab   *tukang becak* pedicab driver

sepeda bicycle

motor motorcycle

Accommodations

Accommodations in Indonesia range from luxury suites costing hundreds of dollars a night to inexpensive dollar-a-night rooms in lodges called *losmen*. Ask the price of a room first, and have a look before checking in. You will have to fill out a registration form and may be asked to pay in advance. Discounts can often be had for the asking. If you are paying extra for air-conditioning, make sure it works before paying.

Indonesians now use the words *cekin* and *cekout*. Check-out time is normally 12 noon and you may be charged for another night if you stay beyond that. Many Indonesians you meet will invite you to stay in their home, and good friends may be offended (or will at least act so) if you pay a visit without spending the night.

hotel hotel	***losmen*** lodge (cheap)
penginapan small hotel (cheap)	
wisma guesthouse (medium priced)	

kamar room	***kunci*** key
bagasi baggage	***kopor*** suitcase
rekening, bon bill	***tarip*** rate, tariff
penuh full	***kosong*** empty, vacant
daftar to register	***titip*** to leave with someone
cekin to check in	***cekout*** to check out
cuci to wash	***bersihkan*** to clean

Masih ada kamar? Are there still rooms available?

Masih. Yes, there still are.

Untuk berapa orang? For how many people?

Untuk tiga orang. For three people.

Ma'af, sudah penuh. I'm sorry, we are already full.

Taripnya berapa?
   What (how much) is the rate?

Ada kamar yang lebih murah?
   Do you have cheaper rooms?

Boleh saya lihat kamar dulu?
   May I see the room first?

Berapa malam tuan/nyonya tinggal di sini?
   How many nights will you stay, sir/ma'am?

Tiga malam. Three nights.

Silahkan daftar dulu. Please register first.

Ini kuncinya. Here is the key.

Kuncinya dititip di kantor kalau keluar.
   Please leave the key in the office if you go out.

The Hotel Panghegar in Bandung, West Java.

Saya mau bayar rekening sekarang.
I want to pay the bill now.

Mas! Tolong ambil bagasi.
Porter! Please take our luggage.

Tolong mas, minta air minum.
Please give us some drinking water.

Ada banyak nyamuk. There are lots of mosquitoes.

Kamarnya tolong disemprot. Please spray the room.

Tolong bersihkan kamar sekarang.
Please clean/make up the room now.

Tolong cuci pakaian ini. Please wash these clothes

Note: Boiled water for drinking is normally supplied in a thermos or in a bottle, and you should never drink water from the tap. A tip (*hadiah*) of Rp500 to Rp1000 is commonly given to a porter or roomboy, depending on the service rendered.

Tourists visiting a village in Lampung, southern Sumatra.

Useful vocabulary

A/C (pronounced *ah-say*) air-conditioning

kipas angin electric fan

bantal pillow

guling bolster pillow (Dutch wife)

handuk towel

kasur mattress

kelambu mosquito netting

selimut blanket

seprei bedsheet

air panas hot water

gayung water ladle, dipper

kamar mandi bathroom

mandi to bathe

gosok to iron, scrub

toalet toilet

kursi chair

lampu light

meja table

tempat tidur bed

Note: Bathrooms in cheaper hotels do not have bathtubs or showers, just a tub of cold water (*bak mandi*) and a ladle (*gayung*). You are not supposed to climb into the tub, but should instead to use the ladle to splash water over yourself while standing outside it. Many hotels also do not have flush toilets, and you have to use the ladle to flush water down the toilet after use.

Sightseeing

Buddhist and Hindu temples, palaces and religious monuments are the hottest attractions in Indonesia. In Java, you should not miss the *kraton* or palaces of Yogya, Solo and Cirebon, or the *wayang kulit* and *wayang wong* puppet and dance performances. In Bali, there are many lovely temples as well as numerous dance performances and temple festivals. On these and other islands you will also find beautiful volcanic scenery and sculpted rice terraces.

kunjungi to visit

nonton to watch, observe (a show, film)

obyek wisata tourist attraction

turis, wisatawan, pariwisata tourist

air terjun waterfall	**cagar alam** nature reserve
danau lake	**telaga** pond
pulau island	**gua** cave
gunung mountain	**gunung api** volcano
hutan forest, jungle	**mata air panas** hot spring
pemandangan panorama, view	

candi ancient temple (Hindu or Buddhist)

benteng fortress	**kraton** palace
kebun binatang zoo	**klenteng** Chinese temple
mesjid mosque	**museum** museum
patung statue	**taman** garden, park
puri Balinese palace	**pura** Balinese Hindu temple

makam, kuburan gravesite

menara tower, lighthouse

peninggalan kuno archeological remains

pertunjukan performance   *tarian* dance

wayang kulit shadow puppet show

wayang wong traditional Javanese theater

Tuan mau kunjungi ke candi Borobudur hari ini?
Do you want to visit Borobudur temple today?

Tidak. Saya mau ke kraton dulu.
No. I want to go to the palace first.

Mari kita nonton tarian.
Let's watch a dance.

Jam berapa ada pertunjukan?
What time is the performance?

Di Pangandaran ada cagar alam.
At Pangandaran there is a nature reserve.

Ada kebon binatang di sini? Tidak.
Is there a zoo here? No.

Traveling by boat in the Riau Islands.

Leisure activities

baca (buku) to read (books)

berjalan, jalan-jalan to walk, go walking

main to play   *renang* to swim

tidur to sleep   *televisi* television

badminton, bulu tangkis badminton

bioskop movie theater, cinema

kolam renang swimming pool

lapangan field, court

lapangan tenis tennis court

tenis tennis   *sepak bola* football (soccer)

pantai beach   *pasir* sand

Saya mau berenang di pantai.
  I am going swimming at the beach.

Anda mau ikut tidak?
  Would you like to come along?

Tidak, saya mau baca buku ini.
  No, I want to read this book.

Ada lapangan tenis di sini?
  Are there tennis courts here?

Buka jam berapa? What time do they open?

Mari kita ke kolam renang.
  Let's go to the swimming pool.

Mari kita nonton di bioskop. Let's go to the cinema.

Apakah ada bioskop dekat sini?
  Is there a cinema near here?

Ada film apa malam ini? What film is playing tonight?

Travel tips

Getting around Indonesia is easy and inexpensive, if often somewhat slow and uncomfortable with all the heat, dust, smoke and crowds. Allow plenty of time to get where you are going, and always expect some delays!

As Indonesians are doing constantly, it is a good idea to ask as many questions (of as many different people) as possible about the destination of a particular bus or train, what time it departs, whether it is late, the route, how long it will take to get there, how much it costs, and so forth. You will find that you receive a wide variety of answers, and by asking a number of times of various people you will (hopefully) get a correct answer.

Many local forms of transportation like buses, minibuses and pedicabs have no posted prices. It is best to ask a disinterested party the approximate price for transportation before you depart. Always have small change handy, and offer what you think is the correct amount to the conductor. He will tell you if it is not enough.

If you and your party are the only passengers in a car, pedicab or minibus, you must bargain and fix a price *before you depart*. State clearly where you are going, and ask the price. The driver may try to wave you into the vehicle, but a price must be agreed upon first or you may end up paying more than you expected later. If you are not sure, ask in your hotel beforehand how much the fare should be.

When bargaining, offer what you feel is a fair amount and then walk away slowly, repeating the amount several times in a friendly way. The driver will usually call you back. In the end, you should expect to pay a bit more because you are a foreigner. And don't expect to get change back from big bank notes!

Chinese food vendors in Tanjung Pinang, on Bintan Island.

PART FIVE

Food and Drink

Dining in Indonesia can be an extraordinarily pleasurable experience, particularly if you are adventuresome enough to sample the local cuisine. The following basic words and phrases are designed to help you read menus and order food in Indonesian restaurants.

rumah makan, restoran restaurant

warung small restaurant, eating stall

makan to eat	*makanan* food
masak to cook	*masakan* cooking, cuisine
minum to drink	*minuman* a drink, drinks

makan pagi breakfast (lit: "eat morning")

makan siang lunch (lit: "eat midday")

makan malam supper (lit: "eat night")

dingin cold	*panas* hot (temperature)
pesan to order	*lagi* more
rekening, bon bill	*daftar* list, menu

Mas! Waiter! (only used on Java)

Mbak! Waitress! (only used on Java)

pisau knife	*garpu* fork
sendok spoon	*piring* plate
gelas glass	*mangkok* bowl

cangkir cup

sumpit chopsticks

tisu paper napkins

Ada masakan Indonesia di sini?
Do you have Indonesian food here?

Boleh lihat daftar makanan?
May [I, we] see the menu?

Saya mau pesan... I would like to order...

satu porsi... one portion of...

setengah porsi... half a portion of...

Minta garpu dan sendok.
Please give me a fork and spoon.

Minta satu lagi. I would like one more.

Ada minuman dingin (dari kulkas)?
Do you have cold drinks (from the refrigerator)?

Kasih satu botol bir dingin.
Give me one bottle of cold beer.

Tidak pakai es. I don't want ice. (lit: "Don't use ice.")

Minta gelas kosong. I would like an empty glass.

Minta bon. I would like the bill.

Note: When eating informally at home, Indonesians normally use the fingers of the right hand without any utensils. You will see people eating this way in streetside stalls or *warung*, sometimes in small restaurants as well. When eating out in restaurants, however, forks and spoons are more commonly used. Table knives are found only in Western restaurants serving dishes like steak, while chopsticks are provided only in Chinese restaurants.

Basic Food Terms

air (pron: "AYE-er") water   *nasi* cooked rice

air minum drinking water   *gula* sugar

keju cheese   *kuah* broth, soup

tahu soybean curds, tofu   *roti* bread

tempe soybean cakes   *telur* egg

mie wheat noodles (usually made with egg)

miehun rice vermicelli   *kue* cake, cookie

Note: Most meals in Indonesia center around rice as the staple. The phrase *makan nasi* "to eat rice" is in fact often used to mean eating in general. Anything without rice is only considered a snack or a light meal. Noodles are a common light lunch or snack and are widely available, especially in Chinese restaurants. *Tahu* and *tempe* are inexpensive meat substitutes made from soybeans. They are now extremely popular in the West because they are high in protein yet low in fat and cholesterol.

Vegetables *Sayuran*

bawang onion   *bawang putih* garlic

bayam spinach   *buncis* green beans

caisin, bak coi Chinese cabbage

jagung corn   *jamur* mushrooms, fungus

kacang beans, nuts   *kacang panjang* long beans

kentang potatoes   *kangkong* water spinach

kapri snowpeas   *kol, sawi* cabbage

selada lettuce   *selederi* celery

timun cucumber   *terong* eggplant, aubergine

tomat tomato   *wortel* carrot

tanpa daging without meat, vegetarian

Meat *Daging*

ayam chicken   **babi** pork

bebek duck   **sapi** beef

kambing mutton   **hati** liver

bakso meatballs (usually beef)

buntut oxtail   **babat** tripe

sate grilled meat on skewers

Seafood *Seafood*

cumi-cumi, sotong cuttlefish, squid

ikan fish

kepiting crab

udang shrimp, prawn

udang besar lobster

tiram oysters

Vegetable sellers in Lombok, the island just east of Bali.

Cooking Terms

bakar grilled, toasted	***kukus*** steamed
goreng to fry, fried	***panggang*** roasted
rebus boiled	***muda*** unripe, young
kering dry	***basah*** wet, fresh

matang well-cooked, ripe, well-done

mentah raw, uncooked, rare

bubur porridge (usually rice, with meat added)

sop clear soup

soto spicy soup (with meat)

Breakfast *Makan pagi*

Breakfast is often included in the price of a hotel room in Indonesia. For breakfast, most Indonesians eat fried rice (*nasi goreng*) or bread (*roti*) with tea or coffee. In restaurants catering for foreigners, eggs and toast are also served, often with fresh fruits and juices.

mentega butter

roti bakar toast (lit: "burned bread")

selé, selai jam

telur dadar scrambled egg

telur goreng fried egg "over easy"

telur mata sapi fried egg "sunny side up"

telur rebus hard boiled egg

telur rebus setengah matang soft boiled egg

Common Menu Items

Most lunch and dinner menus are subdivided into sections containing rice and noodle dishes, meat, seafood, vegetables and drinks. You will usually be given a pad of paper on which to write down your order. Once you have done this, push it to the end of the table or wave it around so the waiter/waitress will come and pick it up.

When you have finished eating, you can ask for the bill by saying *Sudah!* "Already!" In some restaurants, you have to pay the proprietor at the main counter on the way out.

In most Indonesian restaurants, you will find a fairly "standard" menu containing some or all of the following dishes:

ayam goreng chicken stewed in coconut cream and spices, then deep fried

ayam goreng kecap chicken fried with sweet soy sauce

cap cay goreng stir-fried mixed vegetables (with meat)

cap cay kuah mixed vegetable soup (with meat)

fu yung hai Chinese-style omelette (with onions and meat)

gado-gado mixed vegetables with spicy peanut sauce

gudeg ayam young jackfruit and chicken stewed in coconut cream and spices

gulai kambing spicy curried mutton stew

kare ayam chicken curry

kepiting goreng deep-fried crab

kepiting rebus steamed crab

mie bakso Chinese noodles with meatballs

mie goreng fried noodles with meat and vegetables

mie kuah Chinese noodle soup

mie pangsit dumpling (wonton) noodle soup

nasi campur "mixed rice" i.e. rice with several side dishes

nasi goreng fried rice with meat (often with a fried egg)

nasi rames same as *nasi campur*

nasi rawon spicy beef stew with rice

pecel mixed vegetables with spicy peanut sauce

rujak raw vegetable salad with a sweet and spicy sauce

sate ayam chicken satay

sate kambing mutton satay

sayur asam sour vegetable soup (with baby corn, green beans, eggplant, peanuts, jackfruit nuts)

sayur lodeh vegetables stewed in coconut milk

soto ayam spicy chicken soup (with rice or noodles)

udang goreng mentega prawns stir-fried in butter

udang rebus steamed prawns

Note: To order any of the above vegetable or egg dishes without meat, place the words "without meat" (*tanpa daging*) after the name of the dish. For example: *cap cay goreng tanpa daging* ("stir-fried mixed vegetables without meat"). If you would like the dish not too spicy hot, you should add the words *tidak pedas* ("not spicy hot") or *tidak pakai lombok* ("don't use chili").

Food carts line the waterfront in Ujung Pandang, South Sulawesi.

Condiments and Snacks

acar pickles	***permen*** candy
garam salt	***gula*** sugar
jahe ginger	***madu*** honey
merica, lada pepper	***cabe, lombok*** chili pepper

emping fried crackers made of *belinjo* nuts

krupuk prawn (or fish) crackers

kecap (manis) (sweet) soy sauce

kacang nuts, beans	***saus kacang*** peanut sauce
sambal chili sauce	***saus tomat*** tomato sauce

sambal terasi chili sauce with fermented prawn paste

Notes: The most common condiments found in Indonesian restaurants are pickles (*acar*), sweet soy sauce (*kecap manis*) and some form of chili sauce (*sambal*). You will also find large containers filled with various types of fried wafers, crackers and cracklings. You may help yourself to the latter, and the waiter will add them to your bill.

Fruit sellers in Ambon.

Fruits *Buah*

anggur grape   *apel* apple

arbei strawberry   *belimbing* starfruit, carambola

durian durian   *jeruk* orange, citrus

jeruk bali pomelo (like a large grapefruit)

jeruk nipis, limau lemon

kelapa coconut   *mangga* mango

nanas pineapple   *nangka* jackfruit

papaya papaya   *pisang* banana

rambutan small, hairy red fruit, like a lychee

semangka watermelon

Note: The variety of fruits in Indonesia is astounding. Some, like durians and mangos are seasonal. Many others, like bananas, papayas and pineapples are available year round. It is fun to poke around in the markets, and also cheaper to buy your fruits here.

Drinks *Minuman*

air botol, aqua bottled water

air es ice water

air jeruk orange juice (sweetened)

es jeruk iced orangeade (sweetened)

air limon lemonade

air minum, air matang drinking water, boiled water

air panas hot water

air setrop water flavored with colored syrup

jus juice   *es jus* iced juice

anggur wine   *bir* beer

kopi coffee (black with sugar)

kopi pahit black coffee without sugar

kopi susu coffee with milk and sugar

kopi susu tanpa gula coffee with milk only

susu milk

susu panas hot sweetened milk

susu coklat panas hot chocolate

es teh ice tea

teh panas hot tea with sugar

teh botol bottled tea

teh pahit hot tea with no sugar

teh susu tea with sugar and milk

kopyor old coconut milk with sugar syrup

es kelapa muda iced young coconut milk with sugar

Lots of drinks, including most soft drinks, are known by their brand names. These include Coca Cola, 7 Up, Sprite, Fanta, Milo, Ovaltine, and so forth. Note that A & W Root Beer is pronounced "Ah-Way."

Most Indonesian drinks—including coffee, tea and fruit juices—come heavily sweetened with sugar. If you want them without sugar, or with only a little sugar, you have to specify this when you order. Coffee and tea are normally served sweet but without milk, so if you want milk you have to add the word *susu*. Finally, you need to specify if you want the drink hot or cold.

pahit bitter

teh pahit black tea without sugar

teh susu panas hot tea with milk and sugar

tanpa gula without sugar

kopi tanpa gula black coffee without sugar

kopi susu tanpa gula coffee with milk but no sugar

es kopi iced black coffee with sugar

gula sedikit a little sugar only

es jeruk gula sedikit iced orange juice with only a
  little sugar

Taste

asam sour	*asin* salty
manis sweet	*pahit* bitter
pedas hot (spicy)	

enak tasty, nice	*kurang enak* not so tasty
lumayan so-so	*rasa* to feel, taste
sedap delicious	*segar* fresh

Ibu suka masakan Indonesia?
  Do you like Indonesian cooking?

Ya, enak sekali. Yes, it is very tasty.

Tidak terlalu pedas untuk Ibu? It's not too hot for you?

Ya, sedikit pedas tapi enak. Yes, a bit hot, but tasty.

Masakan di restoran ini kurang enak.
  The food at this restaurant is not so tasty.

Ya, ayam itu terlalu asin. Yes, the chicken is too salty.

Dan sopnya asam sekali. And the soup is very sour.

Tapi nasi gorengnya sedap!
  But the fried rice is delicious!

Notes on hygiene

It is important to take certain precautions so that your visit to Indonesia will not be marred by serious stomach problems. Intermittent bouts of indigestion or mild diahrrea are to be expected, as your stomach adjusts to new foods and stray bacteria. More serious, however, are intestinal parasites that can be picked up from food and utensils that are not hygienically handled. The following are a few tips.

Eat in restaurants rather than in roadside stalls. The problem with the latter is that they have no running water with which to clean dishes and utensils, and often a single bucket of water drawn from a nearby river or canal is used for this purpose throughout the day.

Never drink water straight from the tap. All drinking water (*air minum*) must be boiled. Even in luxury hotels, where the water is treated, it is not safe to drink. A thermos of boiled

Rambutans for sale in Bandung, West Java.

water or bottles of mineral water (*aqua*) are usually provided by the hotel.

Avoid all uncooked foods, including salads and garnishes served in fancy Western restaurants. Buy fresh fruits and vegetables in the market and clean and peel them yourself rather than purchasing already peeled fruits and vegetables from vendors.

Drink tea or bottled drinks rather than fresh fruit juices and other prepared cold drinks served in restaurants and by vendors. Bottled water is available everywhere in Indonesia, generically known by the brand name *aqua*.

Avoid ice altogether, as it is usually made with unboiled water. This is difficult to do on a hot day, but you should be aware that ice is the most common source of stomach ailments among Indonesians and foreigners alike. Instead, ask for refrigerated bottled drinks (*dingin dari kulkas* = "cold from the refrigerator").

Beware of glasses and utensils that are not well washed. You will always see Indonesians wiping their fork and spoon with a napkin before eating in a restaurant.

If you do get sick, it is best to eat plain white rice (*nasi putih*) with vegetable soup (*sop sayur*), bread or rice porridge (*bubur*) and to drink plenty of hot black tea (*teh pahit*).

Famous jeans shops on Jl. Cihampelas, Bandung.

PART SIX

Shopping

jual to sell

belanja to shop

tawar to make an offer (of money)

tawar menawar to bargain (back and forth)

ambil to take

beli to buy

rugi to lose money

kasih to give

barang goods, item

pasar market

toko store

uang money

tunai, cash cash

harga price

harga pas the right price, fixed price

mahal expensive

murah cheap, inexpensive

biasa usual, normal

desain design, pattern

warna color

macam type, kind

istimewa special, "the best"

muda young, light (of colors)

tua old, dark (of colors)

sekali very

mutu, kwalitet quality

terlalu too, excesive

Aduh! My goodness! (expression of shock, dismay)

Colors *Warna-warni*

abu-abu gray	*biru* blue
coklat brown	*hijau* green
hitam black	*kuning* yellow
merah red	*putih* white

The following is a typical shopping scenario, in which a foreigner (F) enters a shop and is waited on by a shop-keeper (S).

S: *Boleh saya bantu?* May I help you?

  Nyonya/Tuan cari apa? What is ma'am/sir looking for?

F: *Lihat-lihat saja.* Just looking.

F: *Harga ini berapa, pak/ibu?*
  What is the price of this, pak/ibu?

S: *Delapan ribu rupiah.*
  Rp8000. (Rp = rupiah)

F: *Aduh! Mahal sekali!*
  My goodness! Very expensive!

S: *Tidak, nyonya. Tidak mahal.*
  No, madam. It's not expensive.

  Lihat kwalitetnya. Look at the quality.

F: *Ya, tapi terlalu mahal.* Yes, but it is too expensive.

S: *Ya, boleh kurang.* Yes, [the price] can be reduced.

  Tuan/nyonya tawar berapa?
  How much does sir/madam offer?

F: *Tiga ribu rupiah boleh?* Is Rp3000 okay?

S: *Tidak, tuan/nonya. Saya rugi.*
  No, sir/ma'am. I will lose money.

  Lima ribu rupiah saja. Rp5000 only.

F: *Aduh! Masih terlalu mahal!*
    My goodness! Still too expensive!

    Empat ribu, itu sudah harga pas.
    Rp4000, that is the normal price.

S: *Ya, boleh.* Yes, okay.

    Tuan/nyonya mau ambil yang mana?
    Which one does sir/ma'am want to take?

F: *Saya mau ini (itu).*
    I want this one/that one.

    Ada warna yang lain?
    Do you have another color?

S: *Ada warna merah, kuning dan hijau.*
    Yes, I have red, yellow and green.

F: *Kasih dua.*
    Give me two.

    Satu merah, satu kuning.
    One red and one yellow.

Street vendors in Yogyakarta, Central Java.

Bargaining

Bargaining is an essential skill in Indonesia. In most shops no fixed prices (*harga pas*) are posted, and it is assumed that bargaining is the rule. This is true in markets and most small shops, as well as for most services. The degree of bargaining required, and the difference between prices normally asked and prices paid, can vary widely.

As a general rule, most Indonesians will never settle for less than a 10% reduction from an asking price. In many cases, however, the asking price may be several times what one normally expects to pay in the end. It simply depends on the situation.

The only places where you don't bargain are in large departmental stores, supermarkets, restaurants and other establishments that clearly display prices. Even then, however, bargaining for large, costly items can often result in lower prices. (People don't usually bargain over very small amounts, except in the market.)

Be especially wary in souvenir and art shops catering for

Souvenirs for sale at Tangkuban Perahu volcano, West Java.

the tourist trade. Here, it is standard practice to mark up astronomically (often five to ten times the normal price), so as to be able to offer huge discounts to unsuspecting tourists, many of whom are then fooled into thinking that they are getting a great deal.

In order to bargain successfully it is essential to first get a rough idea of the *harga pas*, the "right price." The best way to find out is to ask an Indonesian or to shop around. In fact, there is no "right price" in any absolute sense, but there is a range of prices that are more or less competitive with what others are charging. Often, as a foreigner, you simply cannot get the lowest prices because you don't have all the bargaining skills at your disposal.

One of the easiest and most straightforward bargaining tactics as a foreigner is to demonstrate right away to the seller that you know roughly what you should pay for an item. You can do this by offering an amount that is 50% to 25% less than the price you expect to pay. The idea is that you start low, the seller starts high, and you then go back and forth several times until you compromise in the middle. Never open with your final offer.

The vendor will feign shock and protest strongly, counteroffering with a much higher price. You must also feign shock and protest, offering a bit more than your initial price. This continues until one of you agrees with the other's offer, or until you reach an impasse. When the latter occurs, state your last price several times and begin to walk away slowly. The seller will then accept your price if it is reasonable.

Treat this entire process not as a confrontation, but as a piece of impromptu theater. There are several important things to keep in mind. First of all, never let on how truly interested you are in an item. Point out its many defects, real or imagined. Above all, keep smiling and keep the exchange friendly. By cajoling and bantering goodnaturedly with the vendor, you will both have a good time and, equally importantly, you can both maintain your sense of face while arriving at a compromise between your opposing positions.

Some foreigners think they can simply walk into a shop and demand to pay a particular price. This doesn't work. You've got to play the game. Under no circumstances should you get angry because you think the price being being asked is too high. Just walk away and shop elsewhere if this is the case.

It is important to understand also that you must follow through on any offer you make, so don't make an offer if you don't intend to buy. You can ask a price out of curiousity, and there is no obligation, but if you make an offer that the seller accepts, you are stuck. Reneging is simply not done in Indonesia, and the seller may rightfully get very angry.

Lastly, be sure that you have agreed on a price before accepting any goods or services. If you simply hop in a pedicab (*becak*) or a taxi without a meter and tell the driver to take you somewhere without agreeing on a price beforehand, etiquette requires that you pay whatever the driver asks on arrival. Even if the amount demanded is outrageous, he is right and it is your fault for not agreeing on a price beforehand. Bargaining has to take place *before* you accept a service or consume a product, not after.

Souvenirs

Handicrafts *Kerajinan*

keris ceremonial dagger **dompet** wallet
kulit leather **lukisan** painting
payung umbrella **tas** bag/purse
wayang kulit flat shadow puppets (from animal hide)

Woodcarvings *Ukiran kayu*

kayu wood **patung** statue, sculpture
ukiran carving **topeng** mask
wayang golek wooden puppets

Textiles *Tekstil*

batik cap hand-printed batik
batik tulis hand-drawn batik
kain cloth (2m) **sarung** sarong (1.5m)
kain ikat ikat (tie-dyed) weavings
taplak meja table cloth
selendang shoulder-cloth for carrying babies, goods

Jewelry *Perhiasan*

emas gold **perak** silver
intan diamonds **giok** jade
batu permata gems **gelang** bracelet
anting-anting earrings **cincin** ring
kalung, rantai necklace, chain

F: **Tolong tanya.** I would like to inquire.
   Kain ini dari mana? Where is this cloth from?

S: **Ini dari Sumatra, bu.** This is from Sumatra, ma'am.

F: **Sumatra di mana.** Where in Sumatra?

S: **Kain ini dari daerah Batak.**
   This cloth is from the Batak region.

F: **Patung ini baru atau tua?** Is this statue old or new?

S: **Kira-kira lima puluh tahun.** About 50 years (old).

Clothing *Pakaian*

baju, kemeja shirt	**blus** blouse
celana dalam underpants	**celana** pants
jaket jacket, windbreaker	**dasi** tie
jas sport jacket	**kaca, cermin** mirror
kaus T-shirt	**kantong** pocket
kaus kaki socks	**kaus tangan** gloves

pakaian clothing
pakaian dalam underwear
pakaian renang swimming suit

pas just right, to fit, be the proper size

rok dress	**sabuk** belt
sapu tangan hankerchief	**selendang** scarf
sepatu shoes	**setelan** suit
sandal sandals, shower thongs	
ukuran measurement, size	**topi** hat

S: *Bapak mau coba sepatu ini?*
   Would you like to try these shoes, sir?

F: *Ya, saya mau coba yang hitam itu.*
   Yes, I want to try those black ones.

S: *Ukuran bapak berapa?*
   What is your size?

F: *Ukuran saya tiga puluh sembilan.*
   My size is 39 (European size).

S: *Ini pak, coba dulu.*
   Here they are, please try them on.

F: *Sepatu ini terlalu kecil.*
   These shoes are too small.

   Ada ukuran yang lebih besar?
   Do you have a larger size?

S: *Ada pak. Sebentar.*
   Yes we do, sir. Just a moment.

F: *Ya, ini sudah pas.*
   Yes, these fit just right.

T-shirts for sale just outside your hotel room.

Sundries

Photography *Fotografi*

afdruk print, photo print   **kamera, tustel** camera
film film   **lensa** lens
film berwarna color film   **rusak** spoiled, broken
membetulkan to repair   **betul** correct, fixed
cuci, mencuci to wash, develop (of film)

Stationery *Alat-alat tulis*

kertas paper   **amplop** envelope
kertas tulis writing paper   **kartu pos** postcard
tulis to write   **stofmap** envelope
pen pen   **perangko** stamps
bloknote notepaper

Reading materials *Bahan bacaan*

buku book
toko buku bookstore
buku petunjuk (wisata) tourist guidebook
kamus dictionary
koran, surat khabar newspaper
koran Inggeris English newspaper
majalah magazine
peta map
roman, novel novel

Toiletries

kertas W.C. toilet paper	*sabun* soap
sikat gigi toothbrush	*sisir* comb
syampo shampoo	*tampon* tampon
tapal gigi toothpaste	*tisu* tissues

F: *Saya mau cuci film ini.*
I would like to develop this film.

S: *Mau diafdruk berapa besar?*
What size would you like the prints?

F: *Saya mau yang besar saja.* I would like large ones.

S: *Seperti ini.* Like this? (pointing)

F: *Ya, betul.* Correct.
Kapan selesai? When will they be ready?

S: *Satu jam lagi.* In one hour.

Balinese *barong* masks on display.

Rice farmers in West Java.

Practical Necessities

Telephone *Telpon*

Telephone service has improved greatly in Indonesia during the past decade, but it is still erratic. Exchanges are overloaded during peak hours. Numbers frequently change. Directory assistance is difficult. Be patient and keep trying; eventually you will get through.

telpon telephone

nomor telpon telephone number

menelpon to telephone

hubungi to contact, call

sambung to connect

saluran, line line, connection

tekan to press, dial (a phone)

kode (pronounced "KO-duh") code

kode negeri country code

kode wilayah area code

pesawat extension number

interlokal long-distance (within Indonesia)

luar negeri overseas

dalam negeri domestic

Note: Indonesians use the English word **Hello!** (spelled and pronounced **Halo!**) when answering the phone.

When you ask to speak to someone, the person answering will normally ask who is calling by saying ***Dari mana, ya?*** (lit: "From where?"). You may either give your name or the place you are calling from.

> ***Halo! Saya ingin telpon ke luar negeri, ke Amerika Serikat.***
> Hello! I would like to call overseas to the United States.

> ***Tolong hubungi nomor ini.*** Please call this number.

> ***Kode wilayah lima satu nol.*** Area code (510).

> ***Nomornya empat nol lima tiga nol lima lima.***
> The number is 405-3055.

> ***Tunggu sebentar.*** Please wait a moment.

> ***Sedang bicara, pak.*** The line is busy, sir.

> ***Sebentar coba lagi, ya.*** Try again in a moment, okay.

> ***Silahkan bicara, pak.*** Please go ahead and speak, sir.

> ***Wah, tidak ada orang!*** Oh dear, there is no one there!

> ***Salurannya putus.*** The line was cut off.

> ***Boleh saya bicara dengan Ibu Suleiman, pesawat empat kosong dua?***
> May I speak to Mrs. Suleiman, extension 402?

> ***Dari mana, ya?*** Who is calling?

> ***Dari Mr. Jones.*** Mr. Jones.

> ***Halo, Bapak Subagio ada di rumah?***
> Hello, is Mr. Subagio at home?

> ***Sedang keluar, bu.*** He is out, ma'am.

> ***Kira-kira kapan kembali, ya?***
> Approximately when will he come back?

Coba telpon lagi jam dua siang.
Please call again at two o'clock this afternoon.

Halo. Ibu Siti ada? Hello. Is Siti there?

Ma'af, salah sambung! Sorry, wrong number!

Bapak tahu nomor yang betul tidak?
Do you know his correct number or not?

Wah, saya tidak tahu. Oh my, I don't know.

Halo. Cari siapa, pak?
Hello. Whom do you wish to speak to, sir?

Cari Pak Affandi. I am looking for Pak Affandi.

Dari mana, ya? Who's calling, please?

Dari teman. It's a friend. (lit: "From a friend.")

Ada. Sebentar saya panggil bapak.
He is in. Just a moment, I will call him.

A Jakarta sculpture depicting a scene from the Mahabharata.

Post Office   *Kantor Pos*

Post offices tend to be rather chaotic in Indonesia, and you will need to be a bit aggressive to get things done quickly. First of all, find out which counters offer the services you want. Then fight your way through the crowd. Most counters sell stamps, but only certain ones will accept parcels, sell money orders, handle Poste Restante, etc. The following are a few helpful tips:

Once you have bought stamps and stuck them onto a letter or package, return the item to the counter and watch as the stamps are cancelled.

Mail is generally more secure and is delivered more promptly from a post office in a big city, so it is advisable to wait if you are in the countryside.

Regular airmail usually takes about two weeks to North America or Europe; express airmail gets there a few days earlier.

Domestic telegrams are very cheap in Indonesia, but must usually be sent from a separate office (*Kantor Telgram.*)

pos post	*giro* postal money order
loket counter	*ongkos* cost
paket parcel	*perangko* stamp
surat letter	*telgram* telegram

melalui by means of, via

pakai to use

pos biasa normal (surface) mail

pos tercatat registered mail

pos udara airmail (overseas)

pos udara ekspres express airmail (overseas)

kilat express mail (domestic only)

kilat khusus special delivery with return receipt

Tolong tanya. I would like to inquire.

Di mana saya bisa beli perangko?
Where can I buy stamps?

Di loket nomor dua atau nomor tiga.
At counters number 2 or 3.

Di mana bisa kirim paket ke luar negeri?
Where can I send a parcel overseas?

Di loket tujuh. At counter 7.

Baiklah! Terimah kasih. Very well! Thank you.

Ma'af, antrean!
Get in line! (i.e. Don't cut in front of me!)

Permisi Ibu, saya mau kirim surat ini ke Australia melalui pos udara.
Excuse me, ma'am. I would like to send this letter to Australia by airmail.

Ongkosnya berapa? What is the cost?

Seribu lima ratus rupiah. Rp1500.

Kalau pakai pos biasa berapa?
How much is it to use surface mail?

Lima ratus saja, tapi satu bulan baru sampai.
Only Rp500, but it will take one month.

Baiklah! Saya pakai pos udara saja.
Very well! I'll use airmail.

Kasih perangko, untuk dua surat dan satu kartu pos.
Give me stamps for two letters and one postcard.

Bank

bank bank	**cabang** branch
uang money	**uang kecil** small change
uang logam coins	**uang kertas** banknotes
uang tunai, kontan cash	
kurs exchange rate	**transfer** to transfer
tukar, menukar to exchange	

Saya mau tukar uang dolar Amerika.
I would like to change American dollars.

Kursnya berapa hari ini?
What is the exchange rate today?

Kursnya dua ribu tiga ratus rupiah.
The rate is Rp2300.

Baiklah. Saya mau tukar seratus dolar.
Very well. I want to change $100.

A cigarette stall in Lampung, Sumatra.

Customs and Police

bagasi baggage, luggage
kopor suitcase
tas handbag
dompet wallet
curi, mencuri to steal
pencopet pickpocket
pencuri thief

pabean, duane customs
bea cukai customs duty
lapor to declare, report
polisi police
kantor polisi police station
formulir forms

At customs:

Bagasi ini punya siapa? Whose luggage is this?

Punya saya pak. It is mine, sir.

Ada apa dalamnya? What is inside?

Pakaian saja, pak. Just clothing, sir.

Tidak ada barang untuk dilaporkan.
I have nothing to declare.

At the police station:

Pak, saya kehilangan tas/dompet.
Sir, I have lost my purse/wallet.

Di mana? Where?

Baru tadi, di setasiun kereta api.
Just now, in the train station.

Apakah Ibu melihat siapa yang ambilnya?
Did you see who took it?

Tidak pak. Barangkali pencopet.
No sir. Probably a pickpocket.

Baiklah! Ini ada formulir. Very well! Here is a form.

Harus diisi dulu. You must fill it out first.

Having to deal with the government bureaucracy in Indonesia can be a rather trying experience. The only recommendations we can make are patience, persistence, asking as many questions as possible, and more patience. If you seem to be having trouble getting something done, ask **Siapa yang bertanggung jawab dalam hal ini?** "Who has responsibility in this matter?" and don't be satisfied until you find the person in charge.

It never does any good to get angry, however. Keep your cool and explain your position firmly and clearly, repeating it several times. Make sure you understand the procedures being applied, and don't expect anything to happen very quickly! The preparation and signing of documents alone can take several days.

Filling out forms *Mengisi formulir*

The following are common entries on immigration and other forms. Note that it is mandatory to report to the local police wherever you are staying the night in Indonesia. Hotels normally do this for you, by sending in a copy of the check-in form.

nama name	**alamat** residence
tanggal date	**umur** age
kelamin sex	**agama** religion

surat keterangan identification papers

pekerjaan occupation

tempat lahir place of birth

kebangsaan nationality

maksud kunjungan purpose of visit

kawin marital status

tanda tangan signature

Health and illness

Sakit is the all-purpose term for "sickness" or "pain", while *obat* is similarly used to denote any type of medicine or treatment. If you are sick, it is easy and inexpensive to consult a doctor and obtain a prescription in Indonesia. Office hours are during the afternoons and evenings, from 4 pm onwards. At other times, and in case of emergency, you are better off going to a hospital. Major hotels have clinics that are often open to outsiders.

Many doctors speak a bit of English. The normal procedure for flu or stomach ailments, however, is to issue antibiotics without running any tests to see what is causing the problem. If you have serious stomach problems, it is better to go directly to a laboratory and give them stool and urine samples. They will then refer you to a doctor if the tests are positive. The other popular form of treatment is *suntik* or injections. Avoid this if possible, however, as the syringes and needles used may not be sterile.

Pharmacies are usually very well stocked, but most brand names are different in Indonesia, so ask your doctor to note down the generic names of any prescription drugs you may require before you leave.

If you are in a hospital for several days, you will need to hire an attendant (*suster, pergasah*) at a reasonable rate to attend to your needs.

sakit sick

sehat healthy

sakit gigi toothache

sakit kepala headache

sakit leher sore throat

sakit perut, maag stomache ache, intestinal distress

parah serious (of illness)

dokter doctor

dokter gigi dentist

rumah sakit hospital

kecelakaan accident

ambulans ambulance

darurat emergency

unit darurat emergency room (in a hospital)

laboratorium laboratory

jururawat nurse

batuk cough

demam fever

diare, berak-berak diarrhea

hamil pregnant

lecet cut

luka injury, injured

muntah vomit

patah tulang broken bone, to break a bone

pilek, masuk angin, flu cold, flu

pusing dizziness, nausea

racun poison

racun makanan food poisoning

obat medicine

apotik drugstore

antibiotik antibiotics

aspirin aspirin

plester bandage

resep prescription

suntik, injeksi injection

Saya sakit. Ada dokter di sini yang bicara bahasa Inggeris?
> I am sick. Is there a doctor here (i.e. nearby) who speaks English?

Saya mau ke rumah sakit. I want to go to the hospital.

Tolong panggil ambulans. Please call an ambulance.

Saya mau beli obat. I want to buy some medicine.

Di mana ada apotik? Where is a pharmacy?

Ini resepnya. Here is the prescription.

Ada obat untuk batuk?
> Do you have cough medicine?

Ada obat untuk pilek?
> Do you have cold medicine?

Ada obat untuk sakit perut?
> Do you have medicine for stomach ailments?

Bon voyage! Selamat jalan!

Parts of the Body

darah blood	*kulit* skin
otot muscle	*tulang* bone
urat tendon	

kepala head	*mata* eyes
pipi cheeks	*rahang* jaw
mulut mouth	*lidah* tongue
gigi teeth	*hidung* nose
rambut hair	*leher* neck
telinga ear	

badan body	*bahu* shoulders
dada chest	*payudara* breasts
pinggang waist	*perut* stomach, belly
punggung back	

lengan arm	*tangan* hand, forearm, wrist
jari tangan fingers	*kuku* nails
kaki leg, foot	*mata kaki* ankle
jari kaki toes	

kemaluan genitals
rahim womb, uterus
buntut rear

Verb and Noun Affixes

Indonesian has many words that are derived from simple roots through the addition of prefixes and suffixes. For example, the word **baik** alone means "good" and serves as the root for **kebaikan** (with prefix **ke-** and suffix **-an**) meaning "goodness." Another example is the verb **tinggal** which by itself means both "to stay" or "to leave." The derived form **meninggal** (with prefix **me-** and substitution of nasal **n** for initial consonant **t-** of the root) means "to die, pass away," whereas the word **meninggalkan** (with added suffix **-kan**) means "to leave behind."

When dealing with derived forms, there are really two separate problems. First of all, you need to know the mechanical rules for adding prefixes and suffixes to root words so that you are able to do this yourself, and to identify roots of words you come across so you can look them up in a dictionary. Second, you need to understand how the addition of these various prefixes and suffixes changes the meaning of a root.

Verb Affixes

The active prefix *me-* (for transitive verbs)

Most transitive verbs (verbs which can take a direct object) may be prefixed by **me-**. This prefix generally does not change the meaning of the root, but merely emphasizes that a verb is being used in an active (as opposed to passive) sense, i.e. that the subject of the verb is the main focus or topic of the sentence.

lihat ⇒ *melihat* to see

Saya sudah melihat Borobudur.
I have already seen Borobudur.

There are a few idiomatic cases where the addition of *me-* dramatically alters the meaning of the root word, as in the example already given above of *tinggal* ("to stay; to leave") ⇒ *meninggal* ("to die, pass away"), where the latter is a shortened form of *meninggal dunia* meaning "to depart the world."

As already mentioned in Part Two: Grammar, the use of such "active verbal prefixes" is often optional, and in colloquial speech the prefix is usually omitted. Note also that this prefix is never used in relative clauses and imperatives.

This active verbal prefix is also used to create transitive verbs out of nouns and adjectives. In this case the root and the prefixed form have quite different, although related, meanings.

kuning yellow ⇒ *menguning* to turn yellow

kipas a fan ⇒ *mengipas* to fan

kunci a key ⇒ *mengunci* to lock

Rules for prefixing *me-*

The prefix *me-* takes five different forms, depending on the first letter of the word that it is prefixed to. You will need to memorize the following rules for this.

1) *meny-* for words beginning with *s-*

siram ⇒ *menyiram* to sprinkle

surat a letter ⇒ *menyurat* to write a letter

2) *mem-* before words beginning with *b-* and *p-*

    beli ⇒ *membeli* to buy

    pakai ⇒ *memakai* to use

3) *men-* for words beginning with *d-*, *j-*, *c-* and *t-*

    dorong ⇒ *mendorong* to push

    jual ⇒ *menjual* to sell

    cuci ⇒ *mencuci* to wash

    tonton ⇒ *menonton* to watch (a movie, show)

4) *meng-* for words beginning with *k*, *g*, *h* or any vowel

    kasih ⇒ *mengasih* to give

    ganggu ⇒ *mengganggu* to disturb

    harap ⇒ *mengharap* to hope

    atur ⇒ *mengatur* to arrange

5) *me-* before all other initial consonants

Note that in the examples given above, the first letters *p*, *t*, *k* and *s* of the root verbs (i.e. voiceless consonants) are dropped when the prefix is added.

The active prefix *ber-* (for intransitive verbs)

The active prefix *ber-* is used with intransitive verbs (those which cannot take a direct object) in much the same way that *me-* is prefixed to transitive verbs. The verb with this prefix has more or less the same meaning as the root, and as with *me-* it is often omitted in everday speech.

    asal ⇒ *berasal* to originate

    bicara ⇒ *berbicara* to speak

    diri ⇒ *berdiri* to stand

kunjung ⇒ *berkunjung* to pay a visit

Saya ingin berkunjung *ke rumah anda.*
I wish to pay a visit to your house.

Kami berasal dari Australi.
We are from Australia.

Note that there are a number of irregular forms.

ajar to teach ⇒ *belajar* to learn

kerja ⇒ *bekerja* to work

When prefixed to an adjective or noun, *ber-* creates an active, intransitive verb that has the meaning "possessing" or "taking the attribute of" that noun or adjective.

besar large ⇒ *berbesar* to grow up

kembang blossom, flower ⇒ *berkembang* to develop, blossom, expand

bahasa language ⇒ *berbahasa* to know or speak a language

pakaian clothing ⇒ *berpakaian* to get dressed, be dressed

kata words ⇒ *berkata* to speak

Saudara berbesar di mana?
Where did you grow up?

Saya tidak berbahasa Indonesia.
I cannot speak Indonesian.

Note that before words beginning with *r*, *ber-* becomes *be-* (which is to say that only one *r* appears in the resulting prefixed form).

renang ⇒ *berenang* to swim

rencana ⇒ *berencana* to plan

The passive prefix *di-*

The opposite of the active prefix **me-** is the passive prefix **di-** which indicates that the object of the verb is the main focus or topic of the sentence. This is very similar to the passive voice in English. (See Part Two: Grammar for more examples with **di-**.)

> *Mobilnya belum dibetulkan.*
> The car has not yet *been repaired.*

> *Kita diundang ke rumah teman.*
> We *have been invited* to a friend's house.

> *Nasinya sudah dimasak.*
> The rice *has* already *been cooked.*

The perfective prefix *ter-*

The prefix **ter-** is used to indicate that an action has already been completed, with the emphasis being on the resultant state or condition of the direct object. As with **di-** the focus or main topic of the sentence is always the object of the verb and not the subject. In fact the subject is often not even mentioned when **ter-** is used. In this case, the subject is either understood or it may be intentionally left ambiguous as to who or what was responsible for the action.

> *kenal* to know, be acquainted ⇒ *terkenal* to be famous, well-known

> *atur* to arrange ⇒ *teratur* to be well organized, neat

> *pakai* to use ⇒ *terpakai* to have been used

This prefix is often used together with the word **sudah** meaning "already."

> *Kamarnya* sudah *terkunci.*
> The room is already locked.

Bon kami sudah *terbayar belum?*
Has our bill been paid yet?

Note: The use of *ter-* as a verbal prefix is distinct from the use of *ter-* with adjectives, in which case it forms a superlative meaning the most, the greatest, etc. (See Part Two: Grammar.)

The factive suffix -*kan*

The verbal suffix -*kan* is a factive suffix that creates transitive verbs out of intransitive verbs as well as nouns and adjectives.

selesai to be finished ⇒ *selesaikan* to finish or settle something

tinggal to stay, to leave ⇒ *tinggalkan* to leave something behind

kata words ⇒ *katakan* to speak, say

pasar market ⇒ *pasarkan* to market (goods, etc.)

betul correct ⇒ *betulkan* to fix, correct

When -*kan* is added to a verb that is already transitive, it emphasizes that the action is being focused on the direct object of the verb.

Tolong memberikan nasi, Mas.
Waiter, please give [me] some rice.

Suffixed forms with -*kan* may be used in an active sense with *me-* (although the latter is often dropped in everyday speech), or in a passive sense with *di-*.

Saya belum menyelesaikan pekerjaan itu.
I haven't finished that work yet.

Kamera ini bisa dibetulkan tidak?
Can this camera be fixed or not?

The dative suffix -*i*

The dative suffix -*i* is added to intransitive verbs and adjectives to create transitive verbs which imply that something is being done to, toward, for the benefit of, or by the subject. It often conveys a strong sense of location or direction.

> *awas* to be careful, alert ⇒ *awasi* to guard, watch over
>
> *datang* to come ⇒ *datangi* to pay a visit to someone
>
> *pinjam* to borrow ⇒ *pinjami* to lend
>
> *dekat* close, nearby ⇒ *dekati* to approach
>
> *hubung* connect ⇒ *hubungi* to contact, get in touch with

Resulting verbs with -*i* can be used both in an active sense with *me-*, and in a passive sense with *di-*.

Saya akan coba menghubungi anda di kantor.
I will try to contact you at the office.

Tolong barang saya diawasi sebentar.
Please look after my things for a moment.

The causative prefix *per-* (with -*i* and -*kan*)

The prefix *per-* is a causative prefix added to adjectives to form transitive verbs.

> *kecil* small ⇒ *perkecil* to reduce, make smaller
>
> *besar* large ⇒ *perbesar* to enlarge
>
> *panjang* long ⇒ *perpanjang* to extend

It is most often used together with the suffixes -*i* and -*kan* to produce transitive verbs that indicate that the subject of the sentence is instrumental in bringing about the action or state intended. The form **memper-** is used in the active sense, while **diper-** is used in the passive sense. The suffix **-i** is most often used with adjectives and intransitive verb roots, while **-kan** is used with transitive verb roots (but also with some adjectives). The usages of **-i** and **-kan** in these constructions are quite irregular and actually vary with different dialects of Indonesian.

> **lihat** to see ⇒ **perlihatkan** to show (something to someone)
>
> **ingat** to remember ⇒ **peringati** to remind (someone of something)
>
> **kenal** to know, be acquainted ⇒ **perkenalkan** to introduce (to someone)
>
> **timbang** to weigh ⇒ **pertimbangkan** to consider
>
> **baik** good, well ⇒ **perbaiki** to improve, fix, repair

Important note

The usages of **-kan**, **-i**, **per-** and **ber-** are actually quite lexicalized, which is to say that the resulting forms with these affixes are fairly irregular and idiomatic. You cannot expect to add these affixes to every verb, noun or adjective in the language and get something that makes sense. Rather than trying to figure out the rules under which one form should used instead of another, you are better off simply learning the resulting verbs with the affixes as separate vocabulary items.

These four verb affixes are therefore quite different from the active, passive and perfective prefixes **me-**, **di-** and **ter**, which may be used quite freely with any verbs (as well as with many nouns and adjectives).

Noun Affixes

There are a number of different ways of producing nouns out of verbs and adjectives, and even from other nouns. These forms are highly idiomatic, and as with many of the verb forms, you will simply have to learn the nouns derived in this way as separate vocabulary items.

The instrumental prefix *pe-*

The instrumental prefix *pe-* is added to nouns or verbs to produce nouns meaning "one who does" something.

> *laut* sea ⇒ *pelaut* sailer
>
> *main* to play ⇒ *pemain* player

Rules for prefixing *pe-*

As with *me-*, the prefix *pe-* takes five different forms depending on the initial letter of the verb or noun it is attached to.

1) *peny-* before words beginning with *s-*

> *sakit* sick, ill ⇒ *penyakit* illness

2) *pem-* before words beginning with *b-* and *p-*

> *beli* to buy ⇒ *pembeli* buyer
>
> *pakai* to use ⇒ *pemakai* user

3) *pen-* for words beginning with *d-, j-, c-* and *t-*

> *dengar* to hear ⇒ *pendengar* listener
>
> *jual* to sell ⇒ *penjual* seller
>
> *curi* to steal ⇒ *pencuri* thief
>
> *tonton* to watch ⇒ *penonton* viewer

4) **peng-** for words beginning with **k**, **g** or any vowel

> **karang** to write ⇒ **pengarang** author
>
> **ganti** to exchange ⇒ **pengganti** replacement
>
> **urus** to arrange ⇒ **pengurus** person in charge

5) **pe-** before all other initial consonants

Note that in the examples given above, the first letters **p**, **t**, **k** and **s** of the root verbs (i.e. voiceless consonants) are dropped when the prefix is added.

The suffix -an

The suffix **-an** is added to verbs to produce nouns.

> **makan** to eat ⇒ **makanan** food
>
> **minum** to drink ⇒ **minuman** a drink
>
> **pinjam** to borrow ⇒ **pinjaman** borrowings
>
> **tegur** to warn ⇒ **teguran** warning
>
> **kenal** to know, be acquainted ⇒ **kenalan** acquaintance

When added to a noun, the suffix **-an** denotes a noun category.

> **sayur** vegetable ⇒ **sayuran** vegetables (as a group, distinct from meats, etc.)

The circumfix pe- + -an

The nominalizing circumfix **pe- + -an** also changes verbs to nouns. There is no essential difference between this and the simple suffix **-an** and their usages are simply idiomatic. In some cases, there are even two nouns, one with and one without **pe-**, having the same meaning.

periksa to inspect ⇒ *pemeriksaan* inspection

terima to receive ⇒ *penerimaan* receipts

bicara to talk ⇒ *pembicaraan* discussions

harap to hope ⇒ *harapan*, *pengharapan* hope, expectation

labuh to drop anchor ⇒ *labuhan*, *pelabuhan* harbor, port

Rules for adding *pe-* here are the same as those given above.

The circumfix *per-* + *-an*

The circumfix *per-* + *-an* is used to produce nouns from certain verbs in place of *pe-* + *-an*. The main difference seems to be that this form has the sense of agency or causation (cf. the causative verb prefix *per-* above), but again, the usages are quite idiomatic and the resulting nouns simply need to be learned individually.

coba to try ⇒ *percobaan* test, attempt

kawin to marry ⇒ *perkawinan* wedding

kembang flower, blossom ⇒ *perkembangan* development

The circumfix *ke-* + *-an*

The circumfix *ke-* + *-an* is added to verbs and adjectives to produce abstract nouns.

ada to be, have, exist ⇒ *keadaan* state, condition

aman secure, safe ⇒ *keamanan* security

nyata clear, evident ⇒ *kenyataan* facts, evidence

baik good, well ⇒ *kebaikan* goodness

besar large ⇒ *kebesaran* size, largeness

Suggestions for Further Study

To improve one's vocabulary the best method is to get into the habit of reading an Indonesian newspaper with a dictionary, looking up all the words you don't know, and writing them down in a notebook. It is then a good idea to make flashcards for yourself, or to frequently refer back to your notebook, in order to commit these words to memory.

The best dictionary is by John M. Echols and Hassan Shadily, *Kamus Indonesia-Inggeris/An Indonesian-English Dictionary*, 3rd ed., revised by John U. Wolff and James T. Collins (Jakarta: Gramedia, 1989), along with the companion volume *Kamus Inggris Indonesia/An English-Indonesian Dictionary* (Jakarta: Gramedia, 1975). Both are readily available in Indonesia, or from Cornell University Press in the United States.

For a more in-depth treatment of Indonesian grammar, with a lot of useful examples and notes, the standard university text is the two-volume set by Yohanni Johns, *Bahasa Indonesia: An Introduction to Indonesian Language and Culture* (Singapore: Periplus, 1992).

English-Indonesian Dictionary

For the sake of clarity, only the most common Indonesian equivalents for each English word have been given below.

In the case of verbs, simple roots are given first, followed by common affixed form(s) with the same meaning, if any. For more on affixation of verbal roots, see Appendix A.

A

able to **bisa**

about (approximately) **kira-kira, sekitar**

about (regarding) **tentang, mengenai**

above, upstairs **di atas**

accident **kecelakaan**

accidently, by chance **kebetulan**

accommodation **penginapan**

accompany, to **ikut, mendampingi**

according to **menurut**

acquainted, to be **kenal, mengenal**

across from **seberang**

act, to **tindak, bertindak**

action **tindakan**

active **giat**

activity **kegiatan**

add to **tambah, menambah**

address **alamat**

admit, confess **akui, mengakui**

advance money, deposit **uang muka**

advance, go forward **maju**

afraid **takut, ngeri**

after **sesudah, setelah**

afternoon (3 pm to dusk) **sore**

afternoon (midday) **siang**

afterwards, then **kemudian**

again **lagi**

age **umur**

agree to do something, to **janji, berjanji**

agree, to **setujui, menyetujui**

agreed! **setuju! jadi!**

agreement **perjanjian, persetujuan**

air **udara**

airplane **pesawat, kapal terbang**

alive **hidup**

all *semua, seluruh, segala*

alley, lane *gang*

allow, permit *biarkan, perbolehkan*

allowed to (= may) *boleh*

almost *hampir*

alone *sendiri, sendirian*

already *sudah*

also *juga*

ambassador *duta besar*

among *antara, di antara*

amount *jumlah, sejumlah*

ancient *kuno*

and *dan*

angle *segi*

angry *marah*

animal *binatang*

annoyed *kesal*

answer the phone *angkat telpon*

answer, response (spoken) *jawaban*

answer, to respond (a letter) *balas, membalas*

answer, to respond (spoken) *jawab, menjawab*

ape *kera, monyet*

appear, to *muncul, memuncul; timbul, menimbul*

appearance, looks *rupa, penampilan*

apple *apel*

approach, to (in space) *mendekati*

approach, to (in time) *menjelang*

approximately *kira-kira, sekitar*

April *april*

area *wilayah, daerah*

arena *gelanggang*

arm, hand *lengan*

army *tentara*

around (approximately) *kira-kira, sekitar*

around (nearby) *dekat*

around (surrounding) *sekeliling, di sekitar*

arrange, to *atur, mengatur; urus, mengurus*

arrangements, planning *perencanaan*

arrival *ketibaan, kedatangan*

arrive, to *tiba, datang*

art *seni*

artist *seniman*

ashamed, embarrassed *malu*

ask about, to *tanyakan, menanyakan*

ask for, request *minta, meminta*

ask, to *tanya, menanya*

assemble, gather *kumpul, berkumpul*

assemble, put together *pasang, memasang*

assist, to *bantu, membantu*

assistance *bantuan*

astonished *kaget, heran*

at *di*

atmosphere, ambience *suasana*

attain, reach *capai, mencapai, sampai, menyampai*

attend, to *hadir*

attitude *sikap*

auction, to *lelang, melelang*

auctioned off *dilelang*

August *agustus*

aunt *bibi, tante*

authority, person in charge *orang yang berwajib*

authority, power *kekuasaan*

automobile *mobil*

available *sedia, tersedia*

available, to make *sediakan, menyediakan*

average (numbers) *rata-rata*

average (so-so, just okay) *lumayan, sedang*

awake, to *bangun, membangun*

awaken, to *membangunkan*

aware *sadar*

awareness *kesadaran*

B

baby *bayi*

back *belakang*

back of *di belakang*

back up, to *mundur, ngatret*

backwards, reversed *terbalik*

bad *jelek*

bad luck *celaka, malang*

bag *tas*

baggage *bagasi, kopor*

ball *bola*

banana *pisang*

bargain, to *tawar, menawar*

base, foundation *dasar*

based on *berdasar*

basic *yang dasar, umum*

basis *dasar*

basket *keranjang*

bath *mandi*

bathe, to take a bath *mandi*

bathroom *kamar mandi, WC* ("way-say")

bay *teluk*

be, exist, have *ada*

beach *pantai*

bean *kacang*

beat (to defeat) *kalahkan, mengalahkan*

beat (to strike) *pukul*

beautiful (of people) *cakap, cantik*

beautiful (of places) *indah*

beautiful (of things) *bagus*

because *karena, sebab*

become, to *jadi, menjadi*

bed *tempat tidur*

bedroom *kamar tidur*

bedsheet *seprei*

beef *daging sapi*

before (in front of) *di depan, di muka*

before (in time) *sebelum*

beforehand, earlier *dulu*

begin, to *mulai, memulai*

beginning *permulaan*

beginning, in the *pada permulaan*

behind *di belakang*

belief, faith *kepercayaan*

believe, to *percaya, yakin*

below, downstairs *di bawah*

belt *sabuk*

best *paling baik, paling bagus*

better *lebih baik, lebih bagus*

between *antara*

bicycle *sepeda*

big (area) *luas*

big (size) *besar*

bill *bon, rekening*

billion *milyar*

bird *burung*

birth, to give *melahirkan*

birthday *hari ulang tahun*

bitter *pahit*

black *hitam*

blanket *selimut*

blood *darah*

blossom *kembang*

blouse *blus*

blue *biru*

boat *perahu*

body *badan, tubuh*

boil, to *merebus*

boiled *rebus*

bone *tulang*

book *buku*

border, edge *perbatasan, pinggir*

bored *bosan*

boring *membosankan*

born *lahir*

borrow, to *pinjam, meminjam*

botanic gardens *kebun raya, taman raya*

both *dua-duanya, keduanya*

bother, disturb *ganggu, mengganggu*

bother, disturbance *gangguan*

boundary, border *perbatasan*

bowl *mangkok*

box (cardboard) *kardos, dos*

box *kotak*

boy *anak laki-laki*

boyfriend *pacar*

bracelet *gelang*

branch *cabang*

brand *cap, merek*

brave, daring *berani*

bread *roti*

break apart, to *bongkar, membongkar*

break down, to (of cars, machines) *mogok*

break off, to *putus*

break up, divorce *cerai*

break, shatter *pecah, pecahkan, memecahkan*

bridge *jembatan*

bring, to *bawa, membawa*

broad, spacious *luas*

broadcast, program *siaran*

broadcast, to *siarkan, menyiarkan*

broken off **putus**

broken, does not work, spoiled **rusak**

broken, shattered **pecah**

broken, snapped (of bones, etc.) **patah**

broom **sapu**

broth, soup **kuah**

brother **saudara**

brother, older **kakak**

brother, younger **adik**

brother-in-law **ipar**

brown **coklat**

brush **sikat**

brush, to **sikat, menyikat, gosok, menggosok**

buffalo (water buffalo) **kerbau**

build, to **bangun, membangun**

building **gedung**

burn, burnt **bakar**

burned down, out **terbakar**

bus **bis**

bus station **terminal bis**

business **bisnis, perdagangan**

businessman **pedagang**

busy, crowded **ramai**

busy, to be **sibuk**

but **tetapi**

butter **mentega**

butterfly **kupu-kupu**

buy **beli, membeli**

C

cabbage **kol**

cabbage, Chinese **caisin**

cake, pastry **kue**

call on the telephone **menelpon**

call, summon **panggil, memanggil**

calm **tenang**

can, be able to **bisa**

can, tin **kaleng**

cancel **batal, membatalkan**

candle **lilin**

candy **permen**

capable of, to be **sanggup**

capture, to **tangkap, menangkap**

car, automobile **mobil**

card **kartu**

care for, love **sayang, mencintai**

care of, to take **mengasuh, mengawasi**

careful! **hati-hati!, awas!**

carrot **wortel**

carry, to **bawa, membawa**

cart (horsecart) **dokar**

cart (pushcart) **grobag, kereta**

carve, to **ukir, mengukir**

carving **ukiran**

cash money **uang tunai, kontan, kash**

cash a check, to **uangkan**

cast, throw out **buang, membuang**

cat *kucing*

catch, to *tangkap, menangkap*

cauliflower *kembang kol*

cave *gua*

celebrate, to *merayakan*

celery *seledri*

center *pusat, tengah*

central *pusat*

ceremony *upacara*

certain *pasti, tentu*

certainly! *memang!*

chain *rantai*

chair *kursi*

challenge *tantangan*

champion *juara*

chance, to have an opportunity to *sempat*

chance, by accident *kebetulan*

chance, opportunity *kesempatan*

change, small *uang kecil*

change, to (conditions, situations, one's mind) *berubah*

change, exchange (money, opinions) *tukar, menukar*

change, switch (clothes, things) *ganti, mengganti*

character *watak*

characteristic *sifat*

chase away, chase out *usir, mengusir*

chase, to *kejar, mengejar*

cheap *murah*

cheat, someone who cheats *penipu*

cheat, to *tipu, menipu*

cheek *pipi*

cheese *keju*

chess *catur*

chest (box) *peti*

chest (breast) *dada*

chicken *ayam*

child *anak*

chili pepper *cabe, lombok*

chili sauce *sambal*

chocolate *coklat*

choice *pilihan*

choose, to *pilih, memilih*

chopsticks *sumpit*

church *gereja*

cigarette *rokok*

cinema *bioskop*

citizen *warga negara*

citrus *jeruk*

city *kota*

clarification *penjelasan*

clarify, to *menjelaskan*

class, category *golongan, tipe*

classes (at university) *kuliah, mata pelajaran*

clean *bersih*

clean, to *bersihkan, membersihkan, bikin bersih*

cleanliness *kebersihan*

clear *jelas, terang*

clear (of weather) *cerah, terang*

clever *cerdik, pintar*

climate *iklim*

climb onto, into *naik*

climb up (of hills, mountains) *mendaki*

clock *jam*

close together, tight *rapat*

close to, nearby *dekat*

close, to cover *menutup*

closed *tutup*

cloth *kain*

clothes, clothing *pakaian*

cloudy, overcast *mendung*

clove *cengkeh*

clove cigarette *kretek*

coarse, to be *kasar*

coconut *kelapa*

coffee *kopi*

cold, flu *pilek, masuk angin, flu*

cold *dingin*

colleague *rekan*

collect payment, to *tagih, menagih*

color *warna*

comb *sisir*

come in, to *masuk*

come on, let's go *ayo, mari*

come, to *datang*

command, order *perintah*

command, to *perintah, memerintah*

company *perusahaan*

compare, to *membandingkan*

compared to *dibandingkan*

compatible *cocok*

compete, to *menyaingi*

competition *saingan*

complain, to *mengeluh*

complaint *keluhan*

complete, finish something *selesaikan, menyelesaikan*

complete, to be *lengkap*

complete, to make *lengkapi, melengkapi*

completed, finished *selesai*

complicated *rumit*

compose, write (letters, books, music) *karang, mengarang*

composition, writings *karangan*

concerning *tentang, mengenai*

condition (pre-condition) *syarat*

condition (status) *keadaan*

confidence *kepercayaan*

confidence, to have *percaya*

confuse, to *keliru*

confused (in a mess) *kacau*

confused (mentally) *bingung*

confusing *membingungkan*

congratulations! *selamat!*

connect together, to *sambung, menyambung*

connection *hubungan, sambungan*

conscious of, to be *sadari, menyadari*

conscious *sadar*

consider (to have an opinion) *anggap, menganggap*

consider (to think over) *timbangkan, pertimbangkan*

consult, talk over with *rundingkan, merundingkan*

contact, connection *hubungan*

contact, get in touch with *hubungi, menghubungi*

continue, to *teruskan, meneruskan*

cook, to *masak, memasak*

cooked, ripe *masak, matang*

cookie *kue*

cooking, cuisine *masakan*

cool *sejuk*

coral rock *batu karang*

corn *jagung*

cost (expense) *ongkos, biaya*

cost (price) *harga*

cotton *kapas*

cough *batuk*

count, reckon *hitung, menghitung*

counter, window (for paying money, buying tickets) *loket*

country *negara*

cover, to *tutup, menutup*

crab *kepiting*

cracked *retak*

cracker, bisquit *biskuit*

crafts *kerajinan*

craftsman *tukang*

crate *peti*

crazy *gila*

criminal *penjahat*

crowded *ramai*

cruel *kejam, bengis*

cry out, to *teriak, berteriak*

cry, to *tangis, menangis*

cucumber *timun*

culture *kebudayaan*

cup *cangkir*

cured,well *sembuh*

custom, tradition *adat*

customer *langganan*

cut, slice *potongan*

cut, to *potong, memotong*

D

dance *tarian*

dance, to *tari, menari*

danger *bahaya*

dangerous *berbahaya*

daring, brave *berani*

dark *gelap*

date (of the month) *tanggal*

daughter *anak perempuan*

daughter-in-law *menantu*

day *hari*

day after tomorrow *lusa*

daybreak *fajar*

dazed, dizzy *pusing*

dead *mati*

debt *utang*

deceive, to *tipu, menipu*

December *desember*

decide, to *memutuskan*

decision *keputusan*

decrease, to *kurang, kurangi, mengurangi*

deer *rusa*

defeat, to *kalahkan, mengalahkan*

defecate, to *buang air besar, berak*

defect *cacat*

degree, level *nilai*

degrees (temperature) *derajat*

delicious *sedap, enak*

demand, to *tuntut, menuntut*

depart, to *berangkat, tinggal, pergi*

depend on, to *tergantung*

deposit, leave behind with someone *titip, menitip*

deposit, put money in the bank *inkaso*

describe, to *gambarkan, menggambarkan*

desire *kemauan, nafsu*

desire, to *ingin, kepingin*

destination *tujuan*

destroy, to *hancurkan, menghancurkan*

destroyed, ruined *hancur*

determined, stubborn *nekad*

develop, to *berkembang*

develop, to (film) *cuci, mencuci*

development *perkembangan*

diamond *intan*

dictionary *kamus*

die, to *mati, meninggal*

difference (discrepancy in figures) *selisih*

difference (in quality) *perbedaan, beda*

different, other *lain*

difficult *sukar, sulit*

dipper, ladle *gayung*

direct, non-stop *langsung*

direction *jurusan, arah*

dirt, filth *kotoran*

dirty *kotor*

disaster, disasterous *celaka*

discrepancy *selisih*

discuss, to *bicarakan, membicarakan*

discussion *pembicaraan*

display *pajangan*

display, to *pajangkan, memajangkan*

distance *jarak*

disturb, to *ganggu, mengganggu*

disturbance *gangguan*

divide, split up *bagi-bagi, membagi*

division *pembagian*

divorce, to *bercerai*

divorced *cerai*

dizzy, ill *pusing*

do not! *jangan!*

do one's best *berusaha*

do, perform an action *melakukan*

doctor *docter*

document, letter *surat*

dog *anjing*

dolphin *lumba-lumba*

done (cooked) *masak, matang*

done (finished) *selesai*

door *pintu*

doubt something, to *ragu-ragu, meragukan*

doubtful *ragu-ragu*

down, to come or go down, get off *turun, menurun*

down, to take down *turunkan, menurunkan*

downtown *pusat kota, tengah kota*

draw, to *gambar, menggambar*

drawer *laci*

drawing *gambar*

dream *impian, mimpi*

dream, to *mimpi, bermimpi*

dress, skirt *rok*

dressed, to get *berpakaian, ganti baju*

drink, refreshment *minuman*

drink, to *minum*

drive, to (a car) *menyopir, setir*

driver *sopir*

drowned *tenggelam*

drug, medicine *obat*

drugstore *apotik*

drunk *mabuk*

dry *kering*

dry (weather) *kemarau*

dry out (in the sun) *jemur*

duck *bebek*

dusk *senja*

dust *debu*

duty (import tax) *bea cukai*

duty (responsibility) *kewajiban, tugas*

E

each, every *setiap, tiap-tiap*

ear *kuping, telinga*

earlier, beforehand *dulu*

early *awal*

early in the morning *pagi-pagi*

Earth, the World *bumi*

earth, soil *tanah*

east *timur*

easy *gampang, mudah*

eat, to *makan*

echo *gema*

economical *hemat*

economy *ekonomi*

edge *pinggir, batas*

educate, to *didik, mendidik*

education *pendidikan*

effort *usaha*

effort, to make an *berusaha*

egg *telur*

eggplant *terong*

eight *delapan*

electric, electricity *listrik*

elephant *gajah*

eleven *sebelas*

embarrassed *malu*

embarrassing **memalukan**

embassy **kedutaan besar (kedubes)**

emergency **darurat**

empty **kosong**

end, tip **ujung**

enemy **musuh**

energy **tenaga**

enlarge, to **besarkan, membesarkan**

enough **cukup**

enter, to **masuk**

entire **seluruh**

entirety, whole **keseluruhan**

envelope **sampul**

envy, envious **iri hati**

equal **seimbang, sama**

equality **keseimbangan, persamaan**

especially **khusus**

establish, set up **mendirikan**

estimate, to **tafsir, menafsir**

ethnic group **bangsa, suku bangsa**

even (also) **juga**

even (smooth) **rata**

ever, have already **pernah**

every kind of **segala macam**

every **tiap, segala**

every time **tiap kali**

exact, exactly **tepat**

exactly! just so! **persis!**

exam, test **ujian**

examine, to **periksa, memeriksa**

example **umpama, misal**

example, for **umpamanya, misalnya**

except **kecuali**

exchange rate **kurs**

exchange, to (money, opinions) **tukar, menukar**

excuse me! **permisi!**

exit **keluar**

expand, grow larger **berkembang**

expect, to **harapkan, mengharapkan**

expect, to **mengharap**

expense **biaya**

expensive **mahal**

expensive **mahal**

expert **ahli**

express, state **ucapkan, mengucapkan**

extend, to **perpanjang, memperpanjangkan**

extremely **sangat**

eye **mata**

eyeglasses **kacamata**

F

face **muka**

face, to **hadapi, menghadapi**

fail, to **gagal**

failure **kegagalan**

fall (season) **musim gugur**

fall, to **jatuh**

false (imitation) **tiruan**

false (not true) *keliru*

falsify, to *tiru, meniru*

family *keluarga*

fan (admirer) *penggemar*

fan (used for cooling) *kipas*

fancy *mewah*

far *jauh*

fart, to *kentut*

fast *cepat, lekas*

fat, grease *lemak*

fat, to be *gemuk*

father *bapak, ayah*

father-in-law *mertua*

fault, to *salahkan, menyalahkan*

fear *takut*

February *februari*

feel, to *rasa, merasa*

feeling *perasaan, rasa*

fertile *subur*

fever *demam*

field, empty space *lapangan*

fierce *galak*

fight over, to *merebut*

fight, to (physically) *bertengkar*

fill, to *isi, mengisi*

film *filem*

filter *saringan*

filter, to *saring, menyaring*

find, to *temukan, bertemu, ketemu*

finger *jari*

fingernail *kuku*

finish off, to *habiskan*

finish *selesaikan, menyelesaikan*

finished (completed) *selesai*

finished (no more) *habis*

fire *api*

fire someone, to *pecat, pecatkan*

first *pertama*

first, earlier, beforehand *dulu*

fish *ikan*

fish, to *pancing, memancing*

fit, to *pas*

fitting, suitable *cocok*

five *lima*

fix, to (a time, appointment) *menentukan*

fix, to (repair) *betulkan, membetulkan*

flag *bendera*

flood *banjir*

floor *lantai*

flour *tepung*

flower *bunga, kembang*

flu *pilek, flu*

fluent *lancar*

flute *suling*

fly (insect) *lalat*

fly, to *terbang, menerbang*

follow along, to *ikut*

follow behind, to *menyusul*

following *berikut*

fond of, to be *sayang, menyayangi*

food *makanan*

foot *kaki*

for *untuk, demi, bagi*

forbid, to *melarang*

forbidden *dilarang*

force *daya*

force, to *paksa, memaksa*

foreign *asing*

foreigner *orang asing*

forest *hutan*

forget about, to *melupakan*

forget, to *lupa*

forgive, to *mengampuni*

forgiveness, mercy *ampun*

forgotten *terlupa*

fork *garpu*

form (shape) *bentuk*

form (to fill out) *formulir*

fortress *benteng*

four *empat*

free of charge *gratis, cuma-cuma*

free of restraints *bebas*

free, independent *merdeka*

freedom *kemerdekaan*

fresh *segar*

Friday *Jumat*

fried *goreng*

friend *kawan, teman*

friendly, outgoing *ramah*

from *dari*

front *depan, muka*

fruit *buah*

fry, to *goreng, menggoreng*

full *penuh*

full, eaten one's fill *kenyang*

fullfill, to *penuhi, memenuhi*

function, to work *jalan, berjalan*

funds, funding *dana*

fungus *jamur*

funny *lucu*

G

gamble *judi, berjudi*

garage (for repairs) *bengkel*

garage (for keeping a car) *garasi*

garbage *sampah*

garden *taman, kebun*

garlic *bawang putih*

gasoline *bensin*

gasoline station *pompa bensin*

gather, to *kumpul, mengumpul*

gender *kelamin*

general, all-purpose *umum*

generally *pada umumnya*

gentle *lembut*

get, receive *dapat, mendapat*

ghost *hantu*

gift *hadiah, kado*

girl *gadis, anak perempuan*

girlfriend *pacar*

give *beri, memberi; kasih, mengasih*

glass (for drinking) *gelas*

glass (material) *kaca*

go along, join in *ikut, mengikuti*

go around *keliling*

go back *balik, berbalik*
go down, get off *turun*
go for a walk *jalan-jalan*
go home *pulang*
go out, exit *keluar*
go *pergi, jalan*
go up, climb *naik*
goal *tujuan*
goat *kambing*
God *Tuhan*
god *dewa*
goddess *dewi*
gold *emas, mas*
gone, finished *habis*
good *baik, bagus*
government *pemerintah*
grand, great *hebat*
grandchild *cucu*
grandfather *kakek*
grandmother *nenek*
grape *anggur*
grass *rumput*
grave *kuburan, makam*
gray *abu-abu*
great, formidable *hebat*
green *hijau*
green beans *buncis*
greet, to receive *sambut, menyambut*
greetings *salam*
grill, to *panggang, memanggang*
grow larger, to *berkembang, membesar*
grow, to (intransitive)

tumbuh, bertumbuh
grow, plant *tanam, menanam*
guarantee *jaminan*
guarantee, to *jamin, menjamin*
guard, to *jaga, menjaga*
guess, to *mengira, tafsir*
guest *tamu*
guide, lead *antar, mengantar*
guidebook *buku petunjuk*

H

hair *rambut*
half *setengah, separuh*
hall *ruang*
hand (also wrist, forearm) *tangan*
handicap *cacat*
handicraft *kerajinan*
handsome *cakap*
hang, to *gantung, menggantung*
happen, occur *terjadi*
happened, what happened? *apa yang terjadi?*
happening, incident *kejadian*
happy *bahagia, gembira*
hard (difficult) *sukar, sulit*
hard (solid) *keras*
hardworking, industrious *rajin*
harmonious *rukun*
hat *topi*
have been, ever *pernah*

have, own, belong to **punya**

he **dia**

head **kepala**

healthy **sehat**

hear, to **dengar**

heart **hati, jantung**

heavy **berat**

help, to **tolong, menolong; bantu, membantu**

her **dia**

here **sini, di sini**

hidden **tersembunyi**

hide, to **menyembunyikan**

high **tinggi**

hill **bukit**

him **dia**

hinder, to **menghambat**

hindrance **hambatan**

history **sejarah**

hit, strike **pukul, memukul**

hold back, to **tahan, bertahan**

hold onto, grasp **pegang, memegang**

hole **lobang**

holiday **libur**

holy **keramat**

home, house **rumah**

honey **madu**

hope, to **harap, berharap**

horse **kuda**

hospital **rumah sakit**

hot (spicy) **pedas**

hot (temperature) **panas**

hot spring **mata air panas**

hour **jam**

house **rumah**

how are you? **apa kabar?**

how many? **berapa banyak?**

how much? **berapa?**

how? **bagaimana?**

human **manusia**

humane **manusiawi**

humorous **lucu**

hundred **ratus**

hungry **lapar**

hurt (injured) **luka**

hurt (to cause pain) **sakit**

husband **suami**

hut, shack **pondok, gubug**

I

I **saya**

ice **es**

if **kalau, jika**

imagine, to **bayangkan, membayangkan**

importance, important matters **kepentingan**

important **penting**

impossible **tidak mungkin**

impression **kesan, pesona**

impression, to make an **mengesankan, mempesonakan**

in (time, years) **pada**

in order that, so that **agar, supaya**

in, at (space) **di**

included, including **termasuk**

increase, to **bertambah, tambah banyak**

indeed! **memang!**

indigenous **asli**

influence **pengaruh**

influence, to **mempengaruhi**

influenze **pilek, flu**

inform, to **terangkan, beri-tahu, memberitahukan**

information **keterangan**

information booth **penerangan**

inhale, to **isap, mengisap**

inject, to **menyuntik**

injection **suntik**

injury, injured **luka**

inside **dalam**

inside of **di dalam**

inspect, to **periksa, memeriksa**

instruct, send to do something **suruh, menyuruh**

insult **penghinaan**

insult someone, to **menghina**

insurance **asuransi**

intend, to **hendak, bermaksud**

intended for **ditujukan kepada**

intention **maksud**

interest (paid to a bank) **bunga**

interest (paid by a bank) **jasa giro**

interesting **menarik**

intersection **simpangan**

into **ke dalam**

invitation **undangan**

invite, to (ask along) **ajak**

invite, to (formally) **undang**

involve, to **melibatkan**

involved **terlibat**

iron **besi**

iron, to (clothing) **gosok, menggosok**

is **adalah, merupakan**

island **pulau**

it **ini, itu**

item **barang**

ivory **gading**

J

jail **penjara**

jam **selai, sele**

January **januari**

jealous **cemburu**

job **pekerjaan, tugas**

join together, to **sambung, gabung**

join, go along **ikut, mengikuti**

journalist **wartawan**

Juli **juli**

jump, to **lompat, melompat**

June **juni**

jungle **hutan**

just now **baru saja, baru tadi**

just, only **cuma, hanya, saja**

K

keep, to **simpan, menyimpan**

key **kunci**

kill, murder **membunuh**

kind, good (of persons) **baik hati**

kind, type **macam, jenis**

king **raja**

kiss **cium, mencium**

kitchen **dapur**

knife **pisau**

knock, to **ketuk, mengetuk**

know, to **tahu**

know, be acquainted with **kenal, mengenal**

knowledge **pengetahuan**

L

ladle, dipper **gayung**

lady **wanita**

lake **danau**

lamb, mutton **daging kambing**

lamp **lampu**

land **tanah**

land, to (a plane) **mendarat**

lane (of a highway) **jalur**

lane (alleyway) **gang**

language **bahasa**

large **besar**

last night **tadi malam**

last **terakhir**

late at night **malam-malam**

late **terlambat, telat**

later **nanti**

laugh at, to **ketawakan, menertawakan**

laugh, to **tertawa, ketawa**

lavish, fancy **mewah**

laws, legislation **undang-undang, hukum**

layer **lapisan**

lazy **malas**

lead (to be a leader) **memimpin**

lead (to guide someone somewhere) **antar, mengantar**

leader **pemimpin**

leaf **daun**

leather **kulit**

leave behind by accident **ketinggalan**

leave behind on purpose **tinggalkan, meninggalkan**

leave behind for safekeeping **titip, menitip**

leave, depart **pergi, berangkat, tinggal**

lecture **ceramah, kuliah**

lecturer (at university) **dosen**

left side **kiri**

leg (also foot) **kaki**

lend, to **pinjami, meminjamkan**

less **kurang**

lessen, reduce **mengurangi**

lesson **pelajaran**

let someone know, to **beritahu, kasih tahu**

let, allow **biar, membiarkan**

letter **surat**

level (even, flat) **rata**

level (height) **ketinggian**

level (standard) **nilai**

license (for driving) **sim, surat ijin mengemudi**

license, permit *ijin*

lie down, to *baring, tidur*

lie, tell a falsehood *bohong*

life *nyawa*

lifetime *kehidupan*

lift *angkat, mengangkat*

light (bright) *terang*

light (lamp) *lampu*

light bulb *bola lampu*

lightning *kilat*

lightweight *ringan, enteng*

like, as *seperti*

like, be pleased by *senang, suka*

line *garis*

line up, to *antre*

list *daftar*

listen *dengar, mendengar*

listen to *dengarkan, mendengarkan*

literature *sastra, kesusastraan*

little (not much) *sedikit*

little (small) *kecil*

live (stay in a place) *tinggal, berdiam*

live (be alive) *hidup*

liver *hati*

load *muatan*

load up, to *muat, memuat*

lock *kunci*

lock, to *mengunci*

locked *terkunci, dikunci*

lodge, small hotel *losmen, penginapan*

lonely *kesepian*

long (time) *lama*

long (length) *panjang*

look after, to *mengawasi, menjaga*

look for, to *cari, mencari*

look out! *awas!*

look, see *lihat, melihat*

lose money, to *rugi*

lose something, to *hilang, kehilangan*

lose, be defeated *kalah*

lost (of things) *hilang*

lost (to lose one's way) *menyasar, kesasar*

love *cinta, rasa sayang*

love, to *mencintai*

low *rendah*

loyal *setia*

luck *untung*

luggage *kopor, bagasi*

M

madam *nyonya*

magazine *majalah*

make, to *buat, membuat; bikin, membikin*

male *laki-laki*

man *pria, orang*

manufacture, to *buatkan, produksikan*

many, much *banyak*

map *peta*

March *maret*

marijuana *ganja*

market *pasar*

market, to *pasarkan, memasarkan*

married *kawin, nikah*

marry, get married *menikah*

mask *topeng*

massage *pijat, massage*

massage, to *memijat*

mat *tikar*

material, ingredient *bahan*

matter, issue *soal, hal*

mattress *kasur*

May *mei*

may *boleh*

maybe *mungkin*

me *saya*

mean (to intend to) *bermaksud*

mean (cruel) *kejam, bengis*

mean, to *berarti*

meaning *arti, maksud*

measure, to *ukur, mengukur*

measurement *ukuran*

meat *daging*

meatball *bakso*

medicine *obat*

meet, to *bertemu, ketemu, jumpa, berjumpa, menjumpai*

meeting *pertemuan, rapat*

member *anggota*

memories *kenang-kenangan*

mention, to *menyebutkan*

mentioned *tersebut*

menu *daftar makanan*

mercy *ampun*

merely *cuma, hanya*

message *pesan*

metal *logam, besi*

method *cara*

meticulous *teliti*

middle, center *tengah*

middle, be in the middle of *sedang*

milk *susu*

million *juta*

mirror *kaca, cermin*

mix, mixed *campur*

modest, simple *sederhana*

moment (in a moment, just a moment) *sebentar*

moment (instant) *saat*

Monday *Senin*

money *uang, duit*

monkey *monyet, kera*

month, moon *bulan*

monument *tugu*

moon, month *bulan*

more (comparative quality) *lebih*

more of (things) *lagi, lebih banyak*

morning *pagi*

mosque *mesjid*

mosquito netting *kelambu*

mosquito *nyamuk*

most (the most of) *paling banyak, terbanyak*

most (superlative) *paling*

most, at most *paling-paling*

mother *ibu*

mother-in-law *mertua*

motorcycle *motor, sepeda motor*

mountain *gunung*

mouse, rat *tikus*

moustache *kumis*

mouth *mulut*

move from one place to another *pindah, memindahkan*

move, to *gerak, bergerak*

movement, motion *gerakan*

movie theater *bioskop*

much, many *banyak*

mushroom *jamur*

must *harus, mesti*

mutton *daging kambing*

mutual, mutually *saling*

my, mine *saya, saya punya*

N

nail (fingernail) *kuku*

nail (spike) *paku*

naked *telanjang*

name *nama*

narrow *sempit*

nation, country *negeri*

nation, people *bangsa*

national *negara*

nationality *kebangsaan*

natural *alamiah*

nature *alam*

naughty *nakal*

nearby *dekat*

neat, orderly *rapi, teratur*

necessary, must *harus, mesti*

neck *leher*

need *keperluan, kebutuhan*

need, to *perlu, butuh*

needle *jarum*

neighbor *tetangga*

nephew, niece *keponakan*

nest *sarang*

net *jaring*

network *jaringan*

never *tidak pernah*

new *baru*

news *kabar, khabar*

newspaper *surat kabar, koran*

next (in line, sequence) *berikut*

next to *di samping, di sebelah*

niece, nephew *keponakan*

night *malam*

nightly *tiap malam*

nine *sembilan*

no, not (of nouns) *bukan*

no, not (of verbs and adjectives) *tidak*

noise *bunyi*

noisy *bising*

non-stop *langsung*

nonsense *omong kosong*

noodles *mie*

noon *siang*

normal *biasa*

normally *biasanya*

north *utara*

nose *hidung*

not *tidak, bukan*

not yet *belum*

note down, to *mencatat*

notes *catatan*

novels *roman*

November *nopember*

now *sekarang*

nude *telanjang*

number *nomor*

O

o'clock *jam*

obey, to *turut, menurut*

occupation *pekerjaan*

ocean *laut, samudra*

October *oktober*

odor, bad smell *bau*

of, from *dari*

off, turn off *mematikan*

off, turned off *mati*

office *kantor*

official, formal *resmi*

officials (government) *pejabat*

often *sering*

oil *minyak*

old (of persons) *tua*

old (of things) *lama, tua*

older brother or sister *kakak*

on (of dates) *pada*

on time *pada waktu*

on, at *di*

on, turn on *hidupkan,*
nyalakan, jalankan

on, turned on *nyala, hidup,*
jalan

once *sekali*

one *satu, se-*

one who, the one which *yang*

onion *bawang*

only *saja, cuma, hanya*

open *buka, terbuka*

open, to *membuka*

opponent *pelawan*

opportunity *kesempatan*

oppose, to *melawan*

opposed, in opposition
berlawanan, bertentangan

or *atau*

orange, citrus *jeruk*

order (command) *perintah*

order (placed for food, goods)
pesanan

order (sequence) *urutan*

order something, to *pesan*

order, to be in sequence *urut,*
berurut

order, to command *perintah,*
memerintah

orderly, organized *teratur, rapi*

organize, arrange *mengatur,*
mengurus, menyelengg-
arakan

origin *asal*

original *asli*

originate, come from *berasal*
dari

other *lain*

out *luar*

out, go out **keluar**
outside **luar, di luar**
over, finished **selesai**
over, to turn **balik**
overcast, cloudy **mendung**
overcome, to **mengatasi**
overseas **luar negeri**
overturned **terbalik**
own, to **memiliki, mempunyai**
oyster **tiram**

P

pack, to **membungkus**
package **bungkus, paket**
paid **lunas**
painful **sakit**
paint **cat**
paint, to (a painting) **melukis**
paint, to (houses, furniture) **cat, mengecat**
painting **lukisan**
pair of, a **sepasang**
palace (Balinese) **puri**
palace (Javanese) **kraton**
panorama **pemandangan**
pants **celana**
paper **kertas**
parcel **paket**
pardon me? what did you say? **kenapa?**
parents **orang tua**
part **bagian**
participate **ikut, mengikuti**

particularly, especially **khususnya**
party **pesta**
pass away, die **meninggal**
passenger **penumpang**
past **lewat, melalui**
patient (calm) **sabar**
patient (doctor's) **pasien**
pay, to **bayar, membayar**
payment **pembayaran**
peace **perdamaian**
peaceful **damai**
peak, summit **puncak**
peanut **kacang tanah**
peel, to **kupas, mengupas**
penetrate, to **tembus, menembus**
people **rakyat**
pepper, black **merica, lada**
pepper, chili **lombok, cabe**
percent, percentage **persen**
performance **pertunjukan**
perhaps, maybe **mungkin**
perhaps, probably **barangkali**
period (end of a sentence) **detik**
period (of time) **jangka waktu, masa waktu**
permanent **tetap**
permit, license **ijin**
permit, to allow **mengijinkan**
person **orang**
personality **watak**
pharmacy **apotik**
pick up, to (someone) **jemput,**

menjemput

pick up, lift (something) *angkat, mengangkat*

pick, choose *pilih, memilih*

pickpocket *pencopet*

pickpocket, to *copet, mencopet*

piece, portion, section *bagian*

pierce, penetrate *tembus, menembus*

pig, pork *babi*

pillow *bantal*

pineapple *nanas*

pity! what a pity! *sayang!*

place *tempat*

place, put *taruh, tempatkan, menempatkan*

plan *rencana*

plan, to *merencanakan*

plant *tanaman*

plant, to *tanam*

plate *piring*

play around *main-main*

play, to *main, memain*

please (go ahead) *silahkan, mari*

please (request for help) *tolong*

please (request for something) *minta*

pocket *kantong, saku*

point (in time) *saat*

point out, to *menunjuk*

point, dot *detik*

poison, poisonous *racun*

police *polisi*

pond *telaga*

pool *kolam*

poor *miskin*

pork, pig *babi*

porpoise *lumba-lumba*

possible *mungkin*

post, column *tiang*

postpone, to *tunda, menunda*

postponed, delayed *tertunda, ditunda*

potato *kentang*

pour, to *tuangkan, menuangkan*

power *kuasa, kekuasaan, kekuatan*

powerful *berkuasa, kuat*

practice *latihan*

practice, to *berlatih, melatih*

prawn *udang*

pray, to *berdoa, sembahyang*

prayer *doa*

pregnant *hamil*

prejudice *prasangka*

prepare, to make ready *siapkan*

prepared, ready *siap*

prescription *resep*

present moment, at the *pada saat ini, sekarang*

presently, nowadays *sekarang, kini*

press, journalism *pers*

press, to *tekan, menekan*

pressure *tekanan*

pretty (of places, things) *indah*

pretty (of women) *cantik*

pretty, very *agak, sangat*

price *harga*

priest *pendeta*

print *cetak*

private *pribadi*

probably *barangkali*

problem *masalah*

produce *buat, menghasilkan, memproduksikan*

profit, luck *untung*

program, schedule *acara*

promise, to *janji, berjanji*

proof *bukti*

prove, to *membuktikan*

public *umum*

publish, to *menerbitkan*

pull, to *tarik, menarik*

pump *pompa*

pure *sempurna*

purse *tas*

push, to *dorong, mendorong*

put into, inside *masukkan, memasukkan*

put together, to *pasang, memasang*

put, to place *taruh, menaruh*

Q

quarter *seperempat*

queen *ratu*

question *pertanyaan*

question, to *tanyakan, menanyakan*

queue up *antre*

quiet *sepi*

quite *agak*

R

rain *hujan*

rain, to *hujan*

raise, lift *angkat*

rank, station in life *pangkat*

ranking *urutan*

rare (scarce) *langka*

rare (uncooked) *mentah*

rarely, seldom *jarang*

rat *tikus*

rate of exchange (for foreign currency) *kurs*

rate, tarif *tarip, ongkos*

rather *agak*

rather than *daripada*

raw, uncooked, rare *mentah*

ray *sinar*

reach *sampai, mencapai*

react, to *menanggapi*

reaction, response *tanggapan*

read *baca, membaca*

ready *siap*

ready, to get *bersiap*

ready, to make *siapkan, menyiapkan*

realize, be aware of *sadari, menyadari*

really! *sungguh!*

rear, tail *buntut*

receive *terima, menerima*

recipe *resep*

recognize, to *kenal, mengenal*

recovered, cured **sembuh**

red **merah**

reduce, to **kurangi, mengurangi**

refined **alus, halus**

reflect, to **mencerminkan**

refuse, to **tolak, menolak**

regarding **terhadap, mengenai**

region **daerah**

register, to **daftar, mendaftar**

registered post **pos tercatat**

registered **terdaftar**

regret, to **menyesal**

regular, normal **biasa**

relax **santai, bersantai**

release, to **lepas, melepaskan**

released **terlepas, dilepas**

religion **agama**

remainder, leftover **sisa**

remains (historical) **peninggalan**

remember, to **ingat**

remembrances **kenang-kenangan**

remind, to **mengingatkan**

rent, to **sewa, menyewa**

rent out, to **sewakan, menyewakan**

repair, to **membetulkan, memperbaiki**

repaired **betul, baik**

repeat, to **ulang, mengulangi**

reply, response **balasan, jawaban**

reply, to (in writing or deeds) **membalas**

reply, to (verbally) **menjawab**

report **laporan**

report, to **lapor, melapor**

request, to (formally) **mohon, memohon**

request, to (informally) **minta**

research **penelitian**

research, to **selidiki, menyelidiki**

reservation **reservasi, pesanan**

reserve, for animals **cagar alam**

reserve, to ask for in advance **pesan dulu**

resident, inhabitant **penduduk**

resolve, to (a problem) **mengatasi, membereskan**

respect **hormat**

respect, to **menghormati**

respond, react **menanggapi**

response, reaction **tanggapan**

responsibility **kewajiban**

responsible, to be **bertanggung jawab**

rest, relax **istirahat**

restrain, to **tahan, tahankan**

restroom **kamar kecil**

result **akibat, hasil**

resulting from, as a result of **disebabkan oleh, karena**

return home, to **pulang**

return (to give back) **mengembalikan**

return (go back) **kembali, balik**

reverse, back up *mundur*

reversed, backwards *terbalik*

rice (cooked) *nasi*

rice (plant) *padi*

rice (uncooked grains) *beras*

ricefields *sawah*

rich *kaya*

rid, get rid of *membuang, menghilangkan*

ride, mount, climb *naik*

right, correct *betul, benar*

right-hand side *kanan*

rights *hak*

ring *cincin*

ripe *matang, masak*

river *kali, sungai*

road *jalan*

roast, grill *panggang*

roasted, grilled, toasted *bakar, panggang*

role *peranan*

room *kamar*

root *akar*

rope *tali*

rotten *busuk*

rough *kasar*

run, to *lari*

S

sacred *keramat*

sacrifice *korban*

sacrifice, to *mengorbankan*

sad *sedih*

safe *selamat*

sail *layar*

sail, to *berlayar*

salary *gaji*

sale *penjualan*

sale (at reduced prices) *obral*

salt *garam*

salty *asin*

same *sama*

sample *contoh*

sand *pasir*

satisfied *puas*

satisfy, to *memuaskan*

Saturday *Sabtu*

sauce *saos*

sauce (chili) *sambal*

save money, to *menghemat*

save, keep *simpan*

say, to *berkata, mengatakan*

scarce *langka*

schedule *jadwal*

school *sekolah*

science *ilmu pengetahuan*

scissors *gunting*

scrub, to *gosok, menggosok*

sculpt, to *pahat, memahat*

sculpture *patung*

sea *laut*

search for, to *cari, mencari*

season *musim*

seat *tempat duduk*

second *kedua*

secret *rahasia*

secret, to keep a *rahasiakan*

secretary *sekretaris*

secure, safe *aman, selamat*

see, to (also observe, visit, read) *lihat, melihat*

seed *biji*

seek, to *cari, mencari*

select, to *pilih, memilih*

self *diri, sendiri*

sell, to *jual, menjual*

send, to *kirim, mengirim*

sentence *kalimat*

separate, to *pisah, memisahkan*

September *september*

sequence, order *urutan*

serious (not funny) *serius*

serious, severe (of problems, illnesses, etc.) *parah*

servant *pelayan, pembantu*

serve, to *melayani*

service *pelayanan, service*

seven *tujuh*

severe (of problems, illnesses, etc.) *parah*

sew, to *jahit, menjahit*

sex, gender *kelamin*

shack *pondok, gubug*

shadow *bayang*

shadow play *wayang kulit*

shake, to (intransitive) *goyang, bergoyang*

shake something, to (transitive) *kocok, mengocok*

shall, will *akan*

shape *bentuk*

shape, to form *membentuk*

sharp *tajam*

shatter, to *pecahkan, memecahkan*

shattered *pecah*

shave, to *cukur, mencukur*

she *dia*

sheep *domba*

ship *kapal*

shirt *baju, kemeja*

shit *berak*

shoes *sepatu*

shop, store *toko*

shop, go shopping *belanja, berbelanja*

short (concise) *ringkas, pendek*

short (not tall) *pendek*

short time, a moment *sebentar*

shoulder *bahu*

shout, to *teriak, berteriak*

show, broadcast *siaran*

show, live performance *pertunjukan*

show, to *menunjukkan, memperlihatkan*

shrimp, prawn *udang*

shut *tutup, menutupi*

sick *sakit*

side *samping*

sign, symbol *syarat*

sign, to *tanda tangani, menanda tangani*

signature *tanda tangan*

signboard *papan, reklame*

silent, quiet *diam, sepi*

silk *sutera*

silver *perak*

simple (easy) *gampang, mudah*

simple (uncomplicated, modest) *sederhana*

since *sejak*

sinews *urat*

sing, to *nyanyi, bernyani*

sir *tuan*

sister *saudara*

sister-in-law *ipar*

sit down, to *duduk*

six *enam*

sixteen *enam belas*

sixty *enam puluh*

size *ukuran, kebesaran*

skewer *tusuk*

skin *kulit*

sky *langit*

sleep, to *tidur*

sleepy *ngantuk*

slow *pelan, lambat*

slowly *pelan-pelan*

small *kecil*

smart *pandai, pintar*

smell, bad odor *bau*

smell, to *cium, mencium*

smile, to *senyum, bersenyum*

smoke *asap*

smoke, to (tobacco) *rokok, merokok*

smooth (to go smoothly) *lancar*

smooth (of surfaces) *rata*

smuggle, to *selundupi, menyelundupi*

snake *ular*

snow *salju*

snowpeas *kapri*

so that *agar, supaya*

so very *begitu*

soap *sabun*

socks *kaus kaki*

soft *empuk, lunak*

sold out *habis*

sold *terjual, laku*

sole, only *tunggal, satu-satunya*

solve, to (a problem) *menye-lesaikan, membereskan*

solved, resolved *beres, selesai*

some *beberapa*

sometimes *kadang-kadang*

son *anak laki-laki*

son-in-law *menantu*

song *lagu*

soon *segera*

sorry, to feel regretful *menyesal*

sorry! *maaf!*

soul *jiwa*

sound *bunyi*

soup (clear) *sop, kuah*

soup (spicy stew) *soto*

sour *asam, kecut*

source *sumber*

south *selatan*

soy sauce (salty) *kecap asin*

soy sauce (sweet) *kecap manis*

space *tempat*

spacious *luas, lapang*

speak, to *bicara, omong*

special *khusus, istimewa*

speech *pidato*

speed *kecepatan, laju*

spend, to *keluarkan, mengeluarkan*

spices *rempah-rempah*

spinach *bayam, kangkong*

spirit *semangat, nyawa*

spoiled (does not work) *rusak*

spoiled (of food) *busuk*

spoon *sendok*

spray, to *semprot, menyemprot*

spring *mata air, sumber*

square (shape) *persegi*

square, town square *alun-alun, padang*

squid *cumi-cumi, sotong*

stamp (ink) *cap*

stamp (postage) *perangko*

stand up, to *berdiri*

star *bintang*

start, to *mulai, memulai*

startled *terkejut*

startling *mengejutkan*

statue *patung*

stay overnight, to *menginap*

stay, to *tinggal, berdiam*

steal, to *curi, mencuri*

steam *uap*

steamed *kukus*

steel *baja*

step *langkah*

steps, stairs *tangga*

stick out, to *tonjol, menonjol*

stick, pole *batang*

stick to, to *melekat, menempel*

sticky *lengket*

stiff *kaku*

still *masih*

stink, to *bau, berbau*

stomach, belly *perut*

stone *batu*

stop by, to pay a visit *mampir*

stop, to *berhenti, stop*

store *toko*

store, to *simpan, menyimpan*

story (of a building) *lantai, tingkat*

story (tale) *cerita*

straight (not crooked) *lurus*

straight ahead *terus, lurus*

strait *selat*

street *jalan*

strength *kekuatan*

strict *ketat*

strike, to go on *mogok kerja*

strike, hit *pukul, memukul*

string *tali*

strong *kuat*

struck, hit *kena*

stubborn, determined *nekad, ngotot*

study, learn *belajar*

stupid *bodoh*

style *gaya*

submerged, drowned *tenggelam*

succeed, to *berhasil*

success *keberhasilan*

suddenly *tiba-tiba*

suffer, to *sengsara*

suffering *kesengsaraan*

sugar *gula*

sugarcane *tebu*

suggest *mengusul, sarankan*

suggestion *usul, saran*

suitable, fitting, compatible
   cocok

suitcase *kopor*

summit, peak *puncak*

sun *matahari*

Sunday *Minggu, Ahad*

sunlight *sinar matahari*

supermarket *toko waserba,*
   supermarket

suppose, to *kira, mengira*

sure *pasti*

surf *ombak*

surface *permukaan*

surprised *heran*

surprising *mengherankan*

suspect, to *mencuriga,*
   menduga, menyangka

suspicion *kecurigaan*

sweat *keringat*

sweep, to *sapu, menyapu*

sweet *manis*

swim, to *berenang*

swimming pool *kolam renang*

swimming suit *pakaian*
   renang

swing, to *goyang, bergoyang*

switch on, turn on *pasang,*
   memasang, nyalakan,
   hidupkan

switch, change *ganti,*
   mengganti

T

t-shirt *kaus*

table *meja*

tail *ekor, buntut*

take *ambil, mengambil*

tall *tinggi*

taste *rasa*

tasty *enak*

tea *teh*

teach, to *ajar, mengajar*

teacher *guru*

team *regu*

teen *belas*

teeth *gigi*

tell, to (a story) *menceritakan*

tell, to (let know) *beritahu,*
   kasih tahu

temple (ancient) *candi*

temple (Balinese-Hindu) *pura*

temple (Chinese) *klenteng*

temple (Indian) *kuil*

temporary, temporarily
   sementara

ten *sepuluh*

tendon *urat*

tens of, multiples of ten
   puluhan

tense *tegang*

test *ujian*

test, to *uji, menguji*

than *daripada*

thank you *terima kasih*

that (introducing a quotation)
   bahwa

that, those *itu*

that, which, the one who *yang*

theater, cinema *bioskop*

their, theirs *mereka punya*

then *lalu, kemudian, lantas*

there *di sana, di situ*

they, them *mereka*

thick (of liquids) *kental*

thick (of things) *tebal*

thief *pencuri*

thin (of liquids) *encer*

thin (of persons) *kurus*

thing *barang, benda*

think, to *pikir, berpikir*

third *ketiga*

thirsty *haus*

thirteen *tiga belas*

this, these *ini*

thoughts *pikiran*

thousand *ribu*

thread *benang*

three *tiga*

through, past *lewat, melalui*

throw out, throw away *buang*

thunder *gemuruh*

Thursday *Kamis*

thus, so *begini, begitu, demikian*

ticket *karcis*

ticket window *loket*

tie, necktie *dasi*

tie, to *tali, mengikat*

tiger *macan*

time to time, once in awhile *sewaktu-waktu*

time *waktu*

times *kali*

tip (end) *ujung*

tip (gratuity) *hadiah, persen*

tired (sleepy) *ngantuk*

tired (worn out) *capai*

title (of books, films) *judul*

title (of persons) *gelar*

to, toward (a person) *kepada*

to, toward (a place) *ke*

today *hari ini*

together *bersama-sama, sekalian*

toilet *kamar kecil*

tomato *tomat*

tomorrow *besok*

tongue *lidah*

tonight *nanti malam*

too (also) *juga*

too (excessive) *terlalu*

too bad! *sayang!*

too much *terlalu banyak*

tool, utensil, instrument *alat*

tooth *gigi*

top *atas*

touch, to *sentuh, menyentuh*

towards *menuju*

towel *handuk*

tower *menara*

town *kota*

trade, business *perdagangan*

trade, to exchange *tukar, menukar*

train *kereta api*

train station *setasiun*

tree *pohon*

tribe *suku*

trouble *kesusahan*

trouble, to *mengganggu, merepotkan*

troublesome *susah, repot*

true *benar, betul*

truly *bersungguh-sungguh*

try *coba, mencoba*

Tuesday *Selasa*

turn around *putar, berputar*

turn off, to *mematikan*

turn on, to *nyalakan, pasang*

turn, make a turn *belok, membelok*

turtle (land) *kura-kura*

turtle (sea) *penyu*

twelve *dua belas*

twenty *dua puluh*

two *dua*

type, sort *macam, jenis*

U

ugly *jelek*

umbrella *payung*

uncle *paman, om*

uncooked *mentah*

under *di bawah*

understand, to *mengerti*

underwear *pakaian dalam*

university *universitas*

unneccessary *tidak usah, tidak perlu*

unripe, young *muda*

until *sampai*

upside down *terbalik*

upstairs *atas, di atas*

urge, to push for *mendesak*

urinate, to *kencing, buang air kecil*

use, to *pakai, memakai, gunakan, menggunakan*

useful, to be *guna, berguna*

useless *tidak berguna, sia-sia*

usual *biasa*

usually *biasanya, pada umumnya*

V

vaccination *suntik*

valid *laku, berlaku*

value *harga*

value, to *hargai, menghargai*

vegetable *sayur*

vegetables *sayuran*

very, extremely *sangat, sekali*

via *melalui, lewat*

view, panorama *pemandangan*

view, to look at *memandang*

village *kampung, desa*

vinegar *cuka*

visit *kunjungan*

visit, to pay a *berkunjung ke, mengunjungi*

voice *suara*

volcano *gunung api*

vomit, to *muntah*

W

wages *gaji*

wait for, to *tunggu, menunggu*

waiter, waitress *pelayan*

wake someone up
   membangunkan

wake up *bangun, membangun*

walk *jalan, berjalan*

wall *tembok, dinding*

wallet *dompet*

want, to *mau*

war, battle *perang*

war, to make *berperang*

warm *hangat*

warn, to *memberi teguran*

warning *teguran*

wash *cuci, mencuci*

watch (wristwatch) *jam tangan*

watch over, guard
   mengawasi, menjaga

watch, to (a show or movie)
   menonton

· watch, look, see *lihat, melihat*

water *air*

water buffalo *kerbau*

waterfall *air terjun*

watermelon *semangka*

wave *ombak*

wax *lilin*

way of, by *melalui*

way, method *cara*

we (excludes the one
   addressed) *kami*

we (includes the one
   addressed) *kita*

weak *lemah*

weapon *senjata*

wear, to *pakai, memakai*

weary *capai, lelah*

weather *cuaca*

weave, to *tenun, menenun*

weaving *tenunan*

Wednesday *Rabu*

week *minggu*

weekly *tiap minggu*

weigh, to *timbang*

weight *berat*

welcome, to *sambut,
   menyambut*

welcome, you're welcome!
   sama-sama! kembali!

well (for water) *sumur*

well, good *baik*

well-cooked, ripe, well-done
   matang

west *barat*

westerner *orang barat*

wet *basah*

what? *apa?*

wheel *roda*

when, at the time *waktu*

when? *kapan?*

where to? *ke mana?*

where? *mana?*

while ago *tadi*

while, awhile *sebentar*

while, during *sambil*

white *putih*

who? *siapa?*

whole, all of *seluruh*

whole, to be complete *utuh*

why? *kenapa?*

wicked *jahat*

wide, width *lebar*

widow *janda*

wife *isteri*

will, shall *mau, akan*

win, to *menang*

wind, breeze *angin*

window *jendela*

wine *anggur*

wing *sayap*

winner *pemenang, juara*

wire *kawat*

with *dengan, sama, beserta*

without *tanpa*

witness *saksi*

witness, to *saksikan, menyaksikan*

woman *perempuan*

wood *kayu*

word *kata*

work on *mengerjakan*

work, occupation *pekerjaan*

work, to function *jalan, berjalan*

work, to *kerja, bekerja*

world *dunia*

worry, to *kuatir, menguatir*

wrap, to *membungkus*

write, to *tulis, menulis, karang, mengarang*

writer *pengarang*

wrong, false *salah*

Y

yawn *ngantuk*

year *tahun*

yell, to *teriak, berteriak*

yellow *kuning*

yes *ya*

yesterday *kemarin*

yet, not yet *belum*

you (familiar) *saudara, engkau, kamu*

you (female) *ibu*

you (male) *bapak*

you're welcome! *kembali, sama-sama*

young, unripe *muda*

younger brother or sister *adik*

youth (state of being young) *peremajaan*

youth (young person) *remaja*

Z

zero *nul, kosong*

zoo *kebun binatang*

Indonesian-English Dictionary

The following is a list of words commonly used in collo-quial, everyday speech. Words borrowed directly from English have generally been omitted since they are read-ily understood by English speakers.

Verbs are normally listed under their root forms, without prefixes or suffixes. Prefixed and suffixed forms are then given only in cases where they are commonly used, and have more or less the same meaning as the simple root form alone. For more information on verbal affixes and derived forms, see Appendix A.

Nouns derived from simple roots have been listed alpha-betically with their respective prefixes and suffixes at-tached, rather than being listed under the root word. This means you don't have to know what the root is, but can simply look up the affixed form.

A

abang older brother

abu-abu gray

acara program

ada to be, have, exist

adat custom, tradition, culture

adik younger brother or sister

agak rather

agama religion

agar in order that, so that

agen agent

ahli expert

air water

air matang boiled water

air minum drinking water

air panas hot spring

air terjun waterfall

ajak to ask along, invite

ajar, mengajar to teach

akan shall, will

akar root

akhir last, end

akibat result

aku I (informal)

akui, mengakui to admit, confess

alam nature

alamat address

alat tool, utensil, instrument

alun-alun town square

alus refined

aman secure, safe

ambil, mengambil to take

ampun forgiveness, mercy

ampuni, mengampuni to forgive

anak child

anak laki-laki son

anak perempuan daughter

anda you (formal)

anggota member

anggur grape, wine

angin wind

angkat, mengangkat to lift, raise up

anjing dog

antar, mengantar to guide, lead

antara among, between

antre to stand in line, queue up

apa kabar? how are you?

apa? what?

apel apple

api fire

apotik pharmacy

arah direction

arti, berarti meaning; to mean

asal, berasal origin; to originate

asam sour

asap smoke

asin salty

asing foreign

asli indigenous, original

atas above, upstairs

atau or

atur, mengatur to arrange, organize

awas! be careful! look out!

ayah father

ayam chicken

ayo come on, let's go

B

babi pork

baca, membaca to read

badan body

bagaimana? how?

bagasi baggage

bagi to divide, share

bagus good

bahagia happy

bahan material, ingredient

bahasa language

bahaya danger, dangerous

bahu shoulder

bahwa that (introduces a quotation or a subordinate clause)

baik good

bajaj three-wheeled minicar

baju shirt

bakar, membakar to burn; roasted, toasted (of food)

bakso meatball

balas, membalas to answer (a letter)

balasan a reply

balik to turn over, go back

banding, dibanding compared to

bandingkan, membanding-kan to compare to

bangsa nationality, people

bangun, membangun awaken; to build

banjir to be flooded, flood

bantal pillow

bantu, membantu to help

banyak many, much

bapak father

barang thing, item

barangkali probably, perhaps

barat west

baru new, just now

basah wet

batal, membatalkan to cancel

batang stick, pole

batas edge, boundary

batu stone

batuk cough

bau smell, odor (bad)

bawa, membawa to carry

bawah below, downstairs

bawang onion

bawang putih garlic

bayam spinach

bayang shadow

bayangkan, membayangkan to imagine

bayar, membayar to pay

bea cukai customs duty

bebas free, unrestrained

bebek duck

beberapa some

becak pedicab

beda, berbeda to differ; difference; to be different

begini thus, so, like this

begitu thus, so, like that

bekerja to work

belajar to study

belakang behind

belanja to shop, go shopping

belas teen

beli, membeli to buy

belok to turn

belum not yet

bemo jitney, minivan, pickup

benang thread

benar true

bendera flag

bengkel garage (for repairs)

benteng fortress

bentuk, membentuk shape; to form

berak shit, to defecate

berangkat to depart

berani brave

berapa? how many? how much?

beras uncooked rice

berat heavy

berdiri to stand up

beres solved, arranged, okay

bereskan, membereskan to solve, arrange

berhenti to stop

beri, memberi to give

berikut next, following

berikutnya the next, the following

berita news

berkembang to develop, expand

bersih clean

bersihkan, membersihkan to clean

berubah to change

besar big

besarkan, membesarkan to enlarge

beserta together with

besi metal, iron

besok tomorrow

betul true, repaired

betulkan, membetulkan to repair, fix

biar! forget about it!

biarkan, membiarkan to allow, let alone, leave be

biasa usual, regular, normal

bibi aunt

bicara, berbicara to speak

biji seed

bikin, membikin to do, make

bilang to say, count

binatang animal

bintang star

bioskop movie theater

biru blue

bis bus

bisa to be able to, can

blus blouse

bodoh stupid

bola ball

boleh to be allowed to, may

bon bill

bongkar to break apart, unpack, disassemble

borong, memborong to buy up

bosan to be bored

bosankan, membosankan to bore

buah fruit, piece

buang, membuang to cast out, throw away

buang air besar defecate

buang air kecil urinate

buat, berbuat, membuat for, do, make

bubur porridge

budaya culture

buka, membuka to open

bukan not, none

bukit hill

bukti proof

buktikan, membuktikan to prove

buku book

bulan month, moon

bumi the earth

buncis green beans

bunga flower

bungkus to wrap; a package

buntut rear, tail

bunuh, membunuh to kill

bunyi, berbunyi a sound; to make noise

burung bird

busuk rotten

c

cabai, cabe chili pepper

cabang branch

cacat defect, handicap

cagar alam nature reserve

cahaya rays

caisin Chinese cabbage

cakap to speak; handsome, pretty

campur mixed; to mix

candi ancient temple, ruins

cangkir cup

cantik beautiful (of women)

cantumkan to mention, include (in writing)

cap brand

capai, mencapai to reach, attain

capai, cape tired, weary

cara way

cari, mencari to look for

cat paint

catat, mencatat to note down

catatan notes

catur chess

celaka bad luck, an accident, disaster

celana pants

cemburu jealous

cepat fast

cerah clear (of weather)

cerai divorced

cerdik clever

cerita story

cermin, mencerminkan mirror; to reflect

cetak, mencetak to print; to score (a goal)

cincin ring (jewelry)

cinta, mencintai love; to love

cita-cita goal, ideal

cium, mencium to kiss

coba, mencoba to try, to try on

cocok to fit, be suitable, match

coklat brown

contoh sample, example

copet to pickpocket; a pickpocket

cuaca weather

cuci, mencuci to wash, develop (of film)

cuka vinegar

cukup enough

cukur to shave

cuma merely

cumi-cumi squid

curi, mencuri to steal

curiga to suspect

D

dada chest

daerah region, district

daftar to register; a list

dagang business

daging meat

dalam inside

dalang puppeteer

damai peace

dan and

dana funds

danau lake

dapat, mendapat to get, reach, attain, find, succeed, be able to do

dapur kitchen

darah blood

darat, mendarat land; to land

dari from, of

daripada than

darurat emergency

dasar basis

datang to arrive, come

daun leaf

daya force

debu dust

dekat near

dekati, mendekati to approach

delapan eight

demam fever

demi for

demikian like that

dendeng meat jerky

dengan with

dengar, mendengar to hear

dengarkan, mendengarkan to listen to

depan front, next

derajat degrees

desa village

desak to urge, push

dewa god

di in, at, on

di atas on top of, above, upstairs

di bawah below, underneath, downstairs

di mana? where?

di- the passive form of verbs

dia he, she, it, him, her

diam, berdiam silent; to be silent

didik, mendidik to educate

dilarang to be forbidden

dinas (government) service

dingin cold

diri, berdiri self; stand, to stand up

dirikan, mendirikan to build, establish

doa prayer

dokar cart

dompet wallet

dorong, mendorong to push

dosen university lecturer

dua two

dua belas twelve

dua puluh twenty

duduk to sit down

duit money (slang)
dulu first, beforehand
dunia world
duta ambassador, emissary

E

ekor tail
emas gold
empat four
enak tasty
enam six
encer thin (of liquids)
engkau you
erat closely related, connected
es ice
esok hari the following day

G

gabung to join together
gading ivory
gadis girl
gado-gado vegetable salad with peanut sauce
gagah strong, dashing
gagal to fail
gajah elephant
gaji wages, salary
galak fierce
gambar picture, drawing, image
gambarkan, menggambarkan to draw; to describe

gampang easy
gang lane, alley
ganggu, mengganggu to disturb, bother
gangguan disturbance
ganja marijuana
ganti, menggantikan to change, switch
gantung to hang
garam salt
garis line
garpu fork
gaya style
gayung ladle, dipper
gedung building
gelang bracelet
gelanggang arena
gelap dark
gelar title, degree
gelas glass
gema echo
gemar to fancy, be a fan of
gembira happy, rejoicing
gemuk fat (of a person)
gerak, bergerak to move
gerakan movement
gereja church
giat active
gigi teeth
gila crazy
golongan class, category
goreng fried
gosok to scrub, brush, iron
goyang to swing, shake
gua cave

gugur wilt, fall (of leaves)

gula sugar

gulai spicy soup

guling to rotate; a bolster pillow

guna, berguna to be useful

guna-guna magical spells

gunakan, menggunakan to make use of

gunting scissors

gunung mountain

gunung api volcano

guru teacher

H

habis gone, finished

habiskan, menghabiskan to finish off

hadapi, menghadapi to face, confront

hadiah gift

hadir to attend

hadirin attendees

hak rights

hak asasi manusia human rights

halus refined

hambat, menghambat to hinder

hambatan hindrance

hamil pregnant

hampir almost

hancur destroyed

hancurkan, menghancurkan to destroy

handuk towel

hangat warm

hantu ghost

hanya only

harap, berharap to hope

harapkan, mengharapkan to expect

harga cost

hari day, day of the week

hari depan in future

hari ini today

harus to be necessary, must

hasil, berhasil result; to succeed

hasilkan, menghasilkan to produce

hati heart, liver

hati-hati! be careful!

haus thirsty

hebat great, formidable

hemat economical

hendak to intend to

henti, berhenti to stop

heran surprised

hidung nose

hidup to live

hijau green

hilang to lose; lost

hilangkan, menghilangkan to get rid of

hina, menghina insulted; to insult

hitam black

hitung to count

hormat respect

hubungan contacts
hubungi to contact
hujan rain; to be raining
hukum law
hutan forest, jungle

I

ia he, she, it (= *dia*)
ibu mother
ijin permit, license
ijinkan, mengijinkan to permit
ikan fish
ikat to tie; handwoven textiles
iklim climate
ikut, mengikuti to follow along, go along
ilmu science, knowledge
imbang equal
indah beautiful (of things, places)
ingat, beringat to remember
ingatkan, mengingatkan to remind
ini this
intan diamond
interlokal long distance telephone
inti essence, core
ipar brother/sister-in-law
iri envious
isap, mengisap to inhale
isi, mengisi to fill

istimewa special
isteri wife
istirahat rest
itu that

J

jadi, menjadi to become, happen
jadwal schedule
jaga, menjaga to guard
jagung corn
jahat wicked
jahit, menjahit to sew
jalan to walk, function; a street or road
jalan-jalan to go out, go walking
jalur lane (of a highway)
jam hour, o'clock
jamin, menjamin to guarantee, assure
jaminan a guarantee, assurance
jamur fungus, mushrooms
janda widow
jangan Do not!
jangka period (of time)
janji, berjanji to promise
jantung heart
jarak distance
jarang rarely
jari fingers
jaring net
jarum needle

jasa service

jatuh to fall

jatuhkan, menjatuhkan to drop

jauh far

jawab, menjawab to answer, reply

jawaban an answer

jelas clear

jelaskan, menjelaskan to clarify

jelek bad, ugly

jembatan bridge

jemput, menjemput to pick up someone

jemur to dry out

jendela window

jenis type, genus

jeruk orange, citrus

jika if, when

jikalau if, when

jiwa soul

jual, menjual to sell

juara champion

judi, berjudi to gamble

judul title of book, article

juga also

Jumat Friday

jumlah amount, total

jumpa, berjumpa, menjumpai to meet

jurusan direction

juta million

K

kabar, khabar news

kaca glass, mirror

kacamata eyeglasses

kacang bean, peanut

kacau confused, messy

kadang-kadang sometimes

kain cloth

kakak older brother or sister

kakek grandfather

kaki leg, foot

kaku stiff

kalah to lose, be defeated

kalahkan, mengalahkan to defeat

kalau if, when, what about? how about?

kali times, occurences; river

kalimat sentence

kamar room

kamar kecil restroom

kamar mandi bathroom

kamar tidur bedroom

kambing lamb, mutton, goat, sheep

kami we

Kamis Thursday

kampung village, hamlet

kamu you

kamus dictionary

kanan right

kangkung a kind of spinach

kantong pocket

kantor office

kapal ship

kapan? when?

kapas cotton

kapri snowpeas

karang, mengarang coral; to write

karangan writings

karcis ticket

karena because

kartu card

kasar coarse

kasih to give, love

kasur mattress

kata, berkata word; to say

kaus t-shirt

kaus kaki socks

kawan friend

kawat wire

kawin to be married

kaya rich

kayu wood

ke to, towards

kebangsaan nationality

kebudayaan culture

kebun garden

kebun binatang zoo

kebun raya botanical gardens

kecap (manis) (sweet) soy sauce

kecelakaan accident

kecil small

kecuali except for

kecut sour

kedua second

kegiatan activity

kejam harsh, tight

kejar, mengejar to chase

keju cheese

kejut, terkejut surprised, startled

kelambu mosquito net

kelamin sex, gender

kelapa coconut

kelenteng Chinese temple

keliling around, to go around

kelilingi, mengelilingi to encircle, go around

keluar to go out, exit

keluarkan, mengeluarkan to spend, put out

keluarga family

keluh, mengeluh to complain

keluhan complaint

kemarau dry (of weather)

kemarin yesterday

kembali to return; you're welcome

kembang blossom

kembangkan, mengem-bangkan to expand

kemudian then, afterwards

kena to hit, be hit, suffer

kenal, mengenal to know, recognize, be acquainted

kenangan memories

kenapa? why? Pardon?

kencing urinate

kental thick (of liquids)

kentang potato

kentut to fart

kenyang full, having eaten enough

kepada to, toward (a person)

kepala head

kepercayaan beliefs, faith

kepiting crab

keponakan niece or nephew

keputusan decision

kera ape

keramat sacred

keranjang basket

keras hard

kerbau water buffalo

kereta api train

keretek clove cigaret

kering dry

keringat sweat

kerja, bekerja work

kertas paper

kesal annoyed, angry

kesan impression

kesempatan opportunity, chance

ketat strict

ketawa laugh

ketemu to find, meet

keterangan information

ketiga third

ketuk to knock

khabar, kabar news

khusus special

kilat lightning

kini nowadays, presently

kipas fan

kipas angin electric fan

kira, mengira to guess, suppose

kira-kira approximately

kiri left

kirim, mengirim to send

kita we

klenteng Chinese temple

kol cabbage

kolam pool

kolam renang swimming pool

kontan cash

kopi coffee

kopor suitcase

koran newspaper

korban sacrifice, victim

kosong empty

kota city, town, downtown

kotak box

kotor dirty

kraton Javanese palace

kuah broth

kuasa power, authority

kuat strong, energetic

kuatir afraid, to worry

kuburan gravesite

kucing cat

kuda horse

kue cake, cookie, pastry

kuku fingernail

kukus steamed

kulit skin, leather

kumis moustache

kumpul gather

kunang-kunang firefly

kunci key, lock

kuning yellow

kunjungan a visit

kunjungi to visit

kuno ancient

kupas, mengupas to peel

kupu-kupu butterfly

kura-kura turtle

kurang less

kurangi, mengurangi to reduce

kurban sacrifice, victim

kurs exchange rate

kursi chair

kurus thin

L

laci drawer

lada pepper

lagi more

lagu song

lahir to be born

lahirkan, melahirkan to give birth

lain different

laju speed

laki-laki male

laku, berlaku sold, valid; to be valid

lakukan, melakukan to do

lalu past; then

lama old (of things); a long time

lambat slow

lampu light, lamp

lancar smooth, proficient, fluent

langganan customer

langit sky

langka scarce

langkah step

langsung directly, non-stop

lantai floor

lantas then

lapang spacious

lapangan field

lapar hungry

lapis layer

lapor, melapor to report

laporan a report

larang, melarang to forbid

lari run, escape

latihan practice

laut sea

lawan to oppose; opponent

layan, melayani to serve (food, etc.)

layar, berlayar a sail; to sail

lebar wide, width

lebih more

lebih banyak more of

leher neck

lekat to stick

lemah weak

lembut gentle

lengan arm

lengkap complete

lepas to release; released

letak to place

lewat to go through, via, past

lidah tongue

lihat, melihat to see, look (also observe, visit, or read)

lilin candle, wax

lima five

limau lemon

limpah to overflow, be overflowing

lindungi to protect

lipat, melipat to fold

listrik electricity

lobang hole

loket ticket window, counter

lombok chili pepper

lompat, melompat to jump

losmen lodge, small hotel

luar outside

luar negeri overseas

luas broad, spacious

lucu funny

luka injury, injured

lukis, melukis to paint

lukisan painting

lumayan so-so, average

lunas paid

lupa to forget; forgotten

lupakan, melupakan to forget about

lurus straight

lusa the day after tomorrow

M

ma'af! sorry!

mabuk drunk

macam kind

macan tiger

madu honey

mahal expensive

main to play

majalah magazine

maju to advance

makam grave

makan to eat

makanan food

maksud, bermaksud meaning, intention; to mean

malam night

malas lazy

malu ashamed, embarrassed

mampir to stop by, visit

mana where

mandi to bathe

mangkok bowl

manis sweet

marah angry

mari please, go ahead, c'mon

masa period

masak to cook

masakan cooking, cuisine

masalah problem

masih still

masuk to come in, enter

masukkan, memasukkan to put inside

mata eye

matahari sun

matang well-cooked, ripe, well-done

mati to die, dead

mau to want

me- active verb prefix

meja table

melalui by way of, via

memang indeed

menang to win

menantu son/daughter-in-law

menara tower, lighthouse

menarik interesting

mendung cloudy

mengerti to understand

meninggal to pass away

meninggalkan to leave behind

mentah raw, uncooked, rare

mentega butter

menurut according to

merah red

merdeka freedom

mereka they, them

merica pepper

mertua father/mother-in-law

mesjid mosque

mesti to be necessary, must

mewah lavish, expensive

mie noodles

miehun rice vermicelli

milik to own

milyar billion

mimpi a dream; to dream

Minggu Sunday

minggu week

minta to ask for, request

minum to drink

minuman drink

minyak oil

miskin poor

mobil car, automobile

mogok to break down (of machines)

mohon to request

motor motorcycle

muat to load, carry, fit inside

muda young, unripe

mudah easy

muka face, across

mulai to start, begin

mulut mouth

muncul to appear

mundur to back up

mungkin maybe, perhaps

muntah to vomit

murah cheap

musim season

musuh enemy

N

naik to ride, go up, climb

nakal naughty

nama name

nanas pineapple

nanti later

nanti malam tonight

nanti sore this afternoon

nasi rice

negara country, nation

nekad determined

nenek grandmother

ngantuk to be sleepy, yawn

nginap, menginap to stay overnight

nikah, menikah to be married, get married

nilai level

nomor number

nul zero

nyala, bernyala to be lit, on

nyamuk mosquito

nyanyi, bernyanyi to sing

nyawa life

nyonya madam

O

obat medicine

obral a sale (at reduced prices)

oleh by

om uncle

ombak wave, surf

omong to speak

omong kosong nonsense

ongkos cost, expense

orang person, human being

orang tua parents

P

pabrik factory

pacar boyfriend or girlfriend

pada on

padang field, square

padi rice plant

pagi morning

paha thigh

pahat, memahat to sculpt

pahit bitter

pajak tax

pajang, memajang to display

pakai, memakai to use, wear

pakaian clothing

pakaian dalam underwear

paket parcel

paksa, memaksa to force

paku nail

paling the most

paling-paling at the most

paman uncle

panas hot (temperature)

pandai smart

pandang, memandang to view

pandangan view, panorama

panggang, memanggang roasted; to roast

panggil, memanggil to call, summon

pangkat rank, station in life

panjang long, length

panjangkan, memanjangkan to extend

pantai beach

parah bad, serious (of illness, problems, etc.)

pasang, memasang to assemble, switch on

pasar a market

pasarkan, memasarkan to market

pasir sand

pasti sure, certain

patah broken (of bones, long objects)

patung statue

payung umbrella

pecah shattered

pecahkan, memecahkan to shatter, break, solve (a problem)

pedagang businessman

pedas hot (spicy)

pegang, memegang to hold, grasp

pejabat civil servant

pekerjaan job, occupation

pelan slow

pelaut sailor

pelayan servant

pelayanan service

pemandangan panoramic view

pemerintah government

pemimpin leader

pencuri thief

pendek short

pendeta priest

penelitian research

pengarang writer

pengaruh influence

penginapan small hotel, accommodation

peninggalan remains

penjara jail

penjelasan clarification

penting important

penuh full

penuhi, memenuhi to fulfill

penumpang passenger

perahu boat

perak silver

peran role

perang war

perangko stamp

perbedaan difference

percaya to believe, have confidence in

perempuan woman

pergi to go, to leave

periksa, memeriksa to examine, inspect

perintah to command; a command

perjanjian agreement

perkembangan development

perlihatkan, memperlihatkan to show

perlu to need

permen candy

permisi! excuse me!

permukaan surface

pernah to have already, have ever

persen percentage, tip

pertama first

pertanyaan question

pertunjukan show, performance

perut stomach, belly

pesan, memesan to order (food, etc.), an order

pesawat airplane, telephone extension, instrument

pesta party

peta map

peti crate

pijat, memijat a massage; to massage

pikir, berpikir to think

pikiran thoughts

pilek a cold, influenza

pilih, memilih to choose, select

pilihan choice

pindah, memindah to move

pinjam, meminjam to borrow

pinjami, meminjami to lend

pintar smart

pintu door

pipi cheek

piring plate

pisah, memisahkan to separate

pisang banana

pisau knife

pohon tree, bush

pompa pump

pompa bensin gas station

pondok hut, shack

potong, memotong to cut; a cut, slice

pria man

pribadi private

puas satisfied

puaskan, memuaskan to satisfy

pukul, memukul to strike

pulang to go back

pulau island

puluh ten, multiples of ten

puncak peak, summit

punya, mempunyai to have, own, belong to

pura Balinese (Hindu) temple

puri Balinese palace

pusat center

pusing dazed, dizzy, ill

putar, berputar to turn around

putih white

putus to break off

putuskan, memutuskan to decide

R

Rabu Wednesday

racun poison

ragu-ragu to be doubtful

rahasia secret

raja king

rajin hardworking, industrious

rakyat people

ramah friendly, open

ramai busy

rambut hair

rantai chain

rapat a meeting; to be close together

rapi orderly, neat

rasa, merasa feeling, taste; to feel

rata even, level

ratu queen

ratus hundred

raya large, great

rayakan, merayakan to celebrate (a holiday)

rebus boiled

rebut to fight about, over

regu team

rekan colleague, workmate

rekening bill

remaja youth

rempah-rempah spices

renang, berenang to swim

rencana, berencana a plan; planned

rencanakan, merencanakan to plan

rendah low

repot troublesome

repotkan, merepotkan to trouble

resep prescription, recipe

resmi official

resmikan, meresmikan to inaugurate, officially open

retak crack, cracked

ribu thousand

ringan light

ringkas concise

roda wheel

rok dress

rokok, merokok cigaret; to smoke

roman novel

roti bread

ruang, ruangan room, hall, space

rugi to lose money

rugikan, merugikan to cause to lose money

rukun harmonious

rumah house, home

rumit complicated

rumput grass

rupa appearance

rusa deer

rusak broken

S

saat moment, instant

sabar patient

Sabtu Saturday

sabuk belt

sabun soap

sadar, menyadari to be conscious, to realize

sahabat friend

saing, bersaing to compete

saingan competition

saja only

sakit sick; painful

saksi witness

saksikan, menyaksikan to witness

sakti sacred power

saku pocket

salah wrong, false

salahkan, menyalahkan to fault

salam greetings

saling mutually

salju snow

sama the same; with, using

sama-sama you're welcome

sambal chili sauce

sambil while

sambung, menyambung to connect

sambungan connection (telephone)

sambut, menyambut to receive, welcome (of persons)

sampah garbage

sampai to arrive, reach; until

samping side

sampul envelope

sana there

sangat very, extremely

sanggup to be capable of, willing to take on

sangka, menyangka suspicion; to suspect

santai, bersantai relax

sapi beef, cow

sapu broom

sarang nest

saring a filter; to filter

sarung sarong, wrap-around skirt

sastra literature

sate barbecued meat on skewers

satu one

saudara brother or sister

sawah rice paddy

saya I, me

sayang to be fond of

sayap wing

sayur, sayuran vegetables

se- prefix meaning one, the same as

sebab because

sebelah next to

sebelas eleven

sebelum before

sebentar in a moment

seberang across from

sebut, menyebut to say

sedang to be in the middle of

sedap delicious

sederhana modest, simple

sedia available

sediakan, menyediakan to prepare, make ready

sedih sad

sedikit little, not much

segala every

segar fresh

segera soon

segi angle, side

sehat healthy

seimbang equal

sejak since

sejarah history

sejuk cool

sekali very; once, one time

sekarang now

sekolah school

sekretaris secretary

selamat congratulations, safe

Selasa Tuesday

selat straits

selatan south

sele, selai jam

seledri celery

selendang shoulder cloth for holding things

selenggarakan, menyelenggarakan to organize

selesai to finish

selidiki, menyelidiki to study, research

selimut blanket

selisih discrepancy

selundup to smuggle

seluruh entire, whole

semangat spirit

semangka watermelon

sembahkan, persembahkan to present

sembahyang to pray

sembilan nine

sembuh cured, recovered

sembunyi to hide; hidden

sementara temporarily

semi to sprout

sempat to have an opportunity to

sempit narrow

semprot, menyemprot to spray

sempurna pure, completed

semua all

senang to like, to be pleased

sendiri self, oneself, alone

sendirian by oneself, all alone

sendok spoon

seni art

seniman artist

Senin Monday

senja dusk

senjata weapon

sentuh, menyentuh to touch

senyum, tersenyum to smile

sepatu shoes

sepeda bicycle

seperempat one quarter

seperti like, as

sepertiga one third

sepi quiet

seprei bedsheet

sepuluh ten

serba all sorts

sering often

serta, beserta with

sesuai dengan adapted to, suited to

sesuaikan, menyesesuaikan to adapt to

sesudah after

setasiún train station

setelah after

setengah half

setia loyal

sewa, menyewa to rent

sewakan, menyewakan to rent out

sia-sia to no avail

siang noon

siap, bersiap ready

siapkan to make ready

siapa? who?

siaran a broadcast, program

sibuk busy

sifat characteristic

sikap attitude

sikat, menyikat a brush; to brush

silakan, silahkan please

simpan, menyimpan to keep, store

simpang, menyimpang to diverge from

simpangan intersection

sinar rays

singkat concise

sini here

sisa leftover, remainder

sisi side, flank

sisir comb

situ over there

soal matter, problem

sop clear soup

sopir driver

sore late afternoon

soto spiced soup

suami husband

suara voice

suasana atmosphere

suatu a certain

subur fertile

sudah already

suhu temperature

suka, menyukai to like

sukar difficult

suku tribe, people

suling flute

sulit difficult

sumpit chopsticks

sumur a well (for water)

sungai river

sungguh really, truly

suntik to inject, vaccinate

supaya in order that, so that

surat letter, document

surat kabar newspaper

suruh, menyuruh to instruct, command

susah difficult

susu milk

susul, menyusul to follow behind

sutra silk

syarat precondition, indication, sign

T

tadi a while ago

tadi malam last night

tafsir, menafsir to guess, to estimate

tagih, menagih to collect payment

tahan to hold back, restrain, survive

tahu to know; soybean curds

(tofu)

tahun year, years

tajam sharp

takut to fear

tali rope, string

taman garden

tamat ended

tambah to add, increase

tamu guest

tanah dirt, land

tanam, menanam to plant, invest

tanaman plant

tanda sign, indication

tanda tangan signature

tangan hand, forearm, wrist

tangga stairs

tanggal date (of the month)

tanggap, menanggap to react

tanggapan reaction, response

tanggung jawab to be responsible, take responsibility

tangis, menangis to cry

tangkap, menangkap to grasp, to capture

tanpa without

tantangan challenge

tante aunt

tanya, bertanya to ask

tari, menari to dance

tarian dance

tarik to pull

tarip tariff, fare

taruh, menaruh to put, place

tas bag, purse

tawar, menawar to make an offer, bargain

tebal thick

tebu sugarcane

tegang tense

tegur to warn

teguran warning

teh tea

tekan to press

tekanan pressure

telaga pond

telanjang naked

telinga ear

teliti meticulous

teluk bay

telur egg

teman friend

tembok wall

tembus, menembus to pierce, penetrate

tempat place

tempat tidur bed

tempe fermented soybean cakes

tempel, menempel to stick

temu, bertemu, menemui to meet

tenaga power

tenang calm

tengah middle

tenggara southeast

tenggelam submerged, drowned

tengok, menengok to see, visit

tentang concerning

tentangan, bertentangan to be opposed, at odds

tentara army

tentu certain, certainly

tentukan, menentukan to fix a time, to establish

tenun, menenun to weave

tenunan weavings

tepat exact, exactly

tepi edge, fringe

tepung flour

terakhir last

terang light, clear, bright

terbang, menerbang to fly

terbit, menerbitkan published; to publish

tercatat registered (post)

tergantung it depends, to depend on

terhadap as regards, regarding, towards

teriak to shout

terima to receive

terima kasih thank you

terjadi to happen; happened

terjun to tumble down

terkejut surprised

terlalu too (excessive)

terlambat late

terminal bus station

terong eggplant, aubergine

tersembunyi hidden

tertawa to laugh

terus straight ahead

teruskan, meneruskan to continue

tetap fixed, permanent

tetapi but

tiang post, column

tiap every

tiba to arrive

tiba-tiba suddenly

tidak no, not

tidak mungkin to be impossible

tidak usah to be not necessary

tidur to sleep

tiga three

tiga belas thirteen

tikar mat

tikus mouse, rat

timbang to weigh

timbangan scale

timbangkan, pertimbangkan to consider

timbul, menimbul to appear, emerge from

timun cucumber

timur east

tindak, bertindak to act

tinggal to depart, live, reside, stay

tinggalkan to leave behind

tinggi tall, high

tingkat level, story of a building

tinjau, meninjau to survey

tipis thin

tipu, menipu to deceive, cheat

tiram oysters

titip to deposit, leave with someone

toko store

tolak, menolak to refuse

tolong, menolong to help, assist

tomat tomato

tonjol, menonjol to stick out

tonton, menonton to watch, observe

topeng mask

topi hat

tua old (of persons)

tuak palm wine

tuan sir

tuang, menuangkan to pour

tubuh body

tugas job, duties

tugu monument

tuju, menuju towards

tujuan destination, goal

tujuh seven

tukang craftsman, tradesman

tukar, menukar to exchange

tulang bone

tulis, menulis to write

tumbuh, bertumbuh to grow (larger, up)

tumbuhan growth

tumbuk to pound

tunai cash

tunda, ditunda to postpone; postponed

tunggal single, sole

tunggu, menunggu to wait, wait for

tunjuk to point out, guide to

tuntut, menuntut to demand

turun to go down, get off

turut to obey

tusuk skewer

tutup, menutup to close, cover

U

uang money

uap steam

ubah, berubah to change

ucapkan, menucapkan to express, say

udang shrimp, prawn

udara air

uji to test

uji coba to try out

ujian test

ujung tip, point, spit (of land)

ukir, mengukir to carve

ukiran carving

ukur, mengukur to measure

ukuran measurement, size

ulang, mengulangi to repeat

ular snake

umpama example

umpamanya for example

umum general, public

umumnya generally

umur age

undang, mengundang invite

undangan invitation

untuk for

untung profit, luck, benefit

upacara ceremony

urat sinews, tendons

urus to arrange

urut to be in sequence

usaha efforts, activities, to try one's best

usir, mengusir to chase away, out

utama most important, chief

utang debt

utara north

utuh whole, complete

warna color

warta berita news

wartawan journalist

warung eating stall, small restaurant

watak character, personality

wayang puppet or dance performance

wayang kulit shadow puppet play

wayang orang traditional Javanese theater

wisma guesthouse

wortel carrot

W

waktu when; time

wanita lady

warga negara citizen

Y

ya yes

yakin to believe

yang the one who, that which